coaching *for* educator wellness

A Guide to Supporting
New and Experienced Teachers

Tina H. Boogren

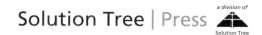
Solution Tree | Press

a division of
Solution Tree

555 North Morton Street
Bloomington, IN 47404
800.733.6786 (toll free) / 812.336.7700
FAX: 812.336.7790

email: info@SolutionTree.com
SolutionTree.com

Visit **go.SolutionTree.com/educatorwellness** to download the free reproducibles in this book.

Printed in the United States of America

Library of Congress Cataloging-in-Publication Data

Names: Boogren, Tina, author.
Title: Coaching for educator wellness : a guide to supporting new and
   experienced teachers / Tina H. Boogren.
Description: Bloomington, IN : Solution Tree Press, 2021. | Includes
   bibliographical references and index.
Identifiers: LCCN 2021006649 (print) | LCCN 2021006650 (ebook) | ISBN
   9781951075798 (paperback) | ISBN 9781951075804 (ebook)
Subjects: LCSH: Teachers--Mental health. | Teachers--Professional
   relationships. | Self-help techniques.
Classification: LCC LB2840 .B657 2021 (print) | LCC LB2840 (ebook) | DDC
   371.102--dc23
LC record available at https://lccn.loc.gov/2021006649
LC ebook record available at https://lccn.loc.gov/2021006650

Solution Tree
Jeffrey C. Jones, CEO
Edmund M. Ackerman, President

Solution Tree Press
President and Publisher: Douglas M. Rife
Associate Publisher: Sarah Payne-Mills
Art Director: Rian Anderson
Managing Production Editor: Kendra Slayton
Copy Chief: Jessi Finn
Production Editor: Miranda Addonizio
Content Development Specialist: Amy Rubenstein
Copy Editor: Mark Hain
Proofreader: Kate St. Ives
Editorial Assistants: Sarah Ludwig and Elijah Oates

This book is dedicated to Brené Brown. Thank you for coaching me from afar with such profound wisdom, vulnerability, and wit. My dream is to share a Topo Chico with you someday.

This book is also dedicated to Tim Kanold. Your mentorship and friendship changed my life in the very best way possible. I pinch myself every single day that we get to pursue our dream—together.

Acknowledgments

I'm sending a special thank-you and huge shout-out to Kosha Patel, Sarah Gates, Teresa Brown, and Deb Boucher. Your gentle guidance and spot-on feedback made this book so much better. Not only are you incredible coaches yourselves, you're also amazing human beings. I'm so grateful for you.

—Tina H. Boogren

Solution Tree Press would like to thank the following reviewers:

Becky Elliott
Assistant Principal
Academy of the Holy Names
Tampa, Florida

Charles Ames Fischer
Education Consultant
Decatur, Tennessee

Alexander Fangman
Principal
Grant's Lick Elementary School
Alexandria, Kentucky

Katie Sheridan
Director, Language and Early Literacy
Kildeer Countryside Community Consolidated School District 96
Buffalo Grove, Illinois

Mary Swanson
District Instructional Coach
ROCORI School District
Cold Spring, Minnesota

Visit **go.SolutionTree.com/educatorwellness** to download the free reproducibles in this book.

Table of Contents

Reproducible pages are in italics.

About the Author

 **Tina H. Boogren, PhD**, is a fierce advocate for educators and an award-winning educator, best-selling author, and highly sought-after speaker. Tina has proudly served as a classroom teacher, mentor, instructional coach, and building-level leader and has presented for audiences all over the world.

Dr. Boogren is deeply committed to supporting educators so that they can support their students. She conducts highly requested and inspiring keynotes, workshops, and virtual webinars that focus on quality instruction, coaching, mentoring, and educator wellness. She also hosts a weekly podcast, *Self-Care for Educators with Dr. Tina H. Boogren*.

Dr. Boogren was a 2007 finalist for Colorado Teacher of the Year and was a recipient of her school district's Outstanding Teacher Award eight years in a row, from 2002 to 2009. She is the author of numerous books, including *In the First Few Years: Reflections of a Beginning Teacher*, *Supporting Beginning Teachers*, *The Beginning Teacher's Field Guide: Embarking on Your First Years*, *180 Days of Self-Care for Busy Educators*, and *Take Time for You: Self-Care Action Plans for Educators*, which was the Independent Publisher's Gold Award winner in the Education category. She is a co-author of *Motivating and Inspiring Students: Strategies to Awaken the Learner* along with Robert J. Marzano, Darrell Scott, and Ming Lee Newcomb and is a contributing author to Richard Kellough's *Middle School Teaching: A Guide to Methods and Resources* and Robert J. Marzano's *Becoming a Reflective Teacher*.

Dr. Boogren holds a bachelor's degree from the University of Iowa, a master's degree with an administrative endorsement from the University of Colorado Denver, and a doctorate from the University of Denver in educational administration and policy studies.

To book Tina H. Boogren for professional development, contact pd@SolutionTree.com.

Introduction

I used to say that I was born to teach. I was the kid who lined my stuffed animals up so I could play teacher, assigning homework and reading stories aloud to them. I also taught tennis lessons and tutored others before I had my own classroom. As I've gotten older and am settling into my own self more and more, I'm realizing that these days, more than being called to *teach*, I'm actually called to *coach*. While teaching and coaching are arguably very similar, I've made a distinction between the two. To me, teaching is about giving someone information or showing someone how to do something: *Here, I know how to do this and you don't yet; let me show you*. I started my career in the classroom, where I taught English language arts to middle school students. My time was spent *teaching* students how to read, write, think, speak, and listen.

Coaching, on the other hand, is about helping people move from where they currently are to where they want to be: *I see your potential; let me nudge you toward it*. In my career, I eventually moved from teaching students to coaching adults. As an instructional coach, I was able to work beside teachers—both new and experienced—as I helped them increase their own expertise. To note, both teaching and coaching are vitally important, necessary, and noble, and the lines certainly get blurred between the two. Today, as an educational consultant, where I'm able to coach educators of all levels, I feel as though I am pursuing the career that I was born to do. Coaching others in order to help them find their own greatness and the greatness in each and every student on their roster is what inspires me to jump out of bed in the morning. This is how I tap into the highest level of Abraham H. Maslow's (1969) hierarchy of needs: transcendence. When I'm coaching, I feel deeply connected to something outside of myself. Having worked hard to become—and stay, at least on most days—self-actualized in terms of both my career and personal wellness, I have an overwhelming desire to help others become self-actualized as well.

Along my journey, I have had the distinct privilege of being coached by some of the best, many of whom I've never even met in person and who don't even know that I exist. Iconic talk show host Oprah Winfrey (n.d.) helped me to become someone who practices gratitude on a daily basis (among other essential lessons). Runner and author Hal Higdon (2005) coached me across the finish line of both the Chicago and New York City marathons. Professor and lecturer Brené Brown (2018) helped me learn that *clear is kind* (saying what we really mean) and taught me how to step boldly into new leadership roles. Author Shawn Achor (2010) trained my brain to become more positive and thus helped me find more success and happiness in my career and life. Author and journalist Elizabeth Gilbert (2015) nudged me toward a more creative life; author and writing teacher Anne Lamott (1994) coached me to write terrible first drafts; and author and ultramarathoner Robin Arzón (2016) convinced me that I *am* an athlete. The list goes on and on, and I am forever grateful that I found these coaches exactly when I needed them.

I've also been honored to have been coached by others in person. These were people who do in fact know me on a personal level. There were mentors and building-level coaches, fellow teachers and professional learning community (PLC) members, assistant principals, principals, directors, superintendents, health coaches, writing instructors, academic advisors, friends, and family members, all of whom helped me get to where I am today. These individuals believed in me before I believed in myself and led by example. They demonstrated to me what a life well lived looks like as an educator, friend, writer, and advocate for personal and workplace wellness.

I've also had the incredible honor of coaching others. As a mentor, instructional coach, and building-level leader, I helped both veteran and novice teachers increase their expertise in a variety of instructional strategies. As a cross-country coach, I helped my middle school runners cross their own finish lines and reach for personal-best times. As a podcaster, I coach listeners in the areas of self-care and educator wellness. Informally, I can't *help* but coach my friends and the educators that I get to work with as a consultant and author. I dare you to nonchalantly mention that you'd like to increase the level of student engagement in your classroom and not see me perk up and lean in, ready to help. Casually announce that there's a 5K that you'd like to run and watch my eyes light up and my toes start tapping. *Pick me! Pick me! Let me help!* At my core, *I believe in the greatness of people* and I truly, truly want to see everyone living *their* very *best* lives because I know the ripple effect that self-actualized people will have on others—particularly their students. And thus, I'm a pusher; that is, a *coach*. I push (coach) because I want to see others become self-actualized in their own lives.

(I'm imagining you, my reader, nodding your head right about now because you recognize these traits in yourself as well.)

I've spent the last few years centering my work around self-care and wellness for educators, hoping to help others—even those I've never met in person—move from where they currently are to where they want to be. I've published books, launched a social media platform and network, started my own podcast, and am co-director of Solution Tree's Wellness Solutions for Educators, all focused on coaching others to become their very best selves. I've also created systems of support for beginning teachers and fine-tuned my own instructional expertise as an associate for both Solution Tree and Marzano Resources. This book is about putting all of those individual pieces together in one place. Here, I'm going to help you fulfill your highest vision for yourself as an instructional coach by helping you consider ways to support both your newest and your most experienced educators as you guide them from where they currently are to where they want to be, both in terms of their instructional expertise *and* in their wellness as professionals. During the COVID-19 pandemic, *more than ever*, we began to understand the requirement for educators to take care of themselves first, so they can in turn take care of their students, both academically and social-emotionally.

As the field of education shifts and stretches and we welcome new methods of reaching each and every learner, we must hold on to the constant ideals: the desire to become self-actualized ourselves and then reach out our hands and help pull the next person up to join us—again and again and again. We cannot—and should not—do this work in isolation. Educators need each other, and as a coach, you can provide that helping hand.

Who This Book Is For

This book is primarily for instructional coaches but will also be beneficial for all instructional leaders, including new teacher mentors and school and district leaders looking to increasing their coaching skills, particularly those who are new to their positions. From my work in the field, I know that instructional coaches and leaders often grapple with how to move from the role of a teacher (of students) to the role of a coach (for adults). They also face challenges regarding how to differentiate their coaching practices for new versus experienced teachers and because of our ever-changing educational landscape are increasingly curious about how to address their teachers' self-care and wellness needs in order to help support students' social-emotional learning needs. I wrote this book to address those needs. This book is meant to help provide guidance and hope in our ever-changing world of education.

Our Road Map

First, I'll help you paint a vivid portrait of *yourself* as an instructional coach. In chapter 1, we'll identify the leadership traits that matter most to you, define your greater why, and outline how to live by your core values. Next, in chapter 2, we'll discover how to build trust in an effective coaching relationship through the essential skills of asking good questions, listening well, providing wait time, paraphrasing, and empathizing. From there, I'll introduce you in chapter 3 to the phases of a typical school year and how understanding each of these phases will help you match your support to what your teachers are currently experiencing. Next, in chapter 4, I'll help you differentiate your support for new teachers, teachers who have previous teaching experience but are new to the building, and experienced teachers by focusing on physical and institutional support. After that, in chapter 5, I'll help you understand how self-care and educator wellness are foundational supports for social-emotional learning for students. Finally, in chapter 6, we'll dig into how supporting all teachers in increasing their expertise and providing instructional support promotes student achievement.

Along the way, you'll have the opportunity to interact with the text through a variety of personal and professional development tools. For example, you'll identify your core values, use a template designed to help combat decision fatigue, and incorporate targeted reflection tools into your coaching conversations. I encourage you to not skip over these invitations, as they are essential to the work of developing your skills as an instructional coach and leader. I also hope that you'll mark up this text in order to engage with it more deeply. Underline ideas that resonate with you, write your own reflections in the margins, and take time to thoughtfully respond to the reflection questions at the end of each chapter.

Whether you're new to the world of coaching or you've been coaching others—formally or informally—for a long time, you are welcome here. While some of the information that I'll share is foundational, familiar, and reaffirming, most of it is fresh and new and presented in a way that addresses teaching's unique challenges of today. I can't wait to share all of this with you. I'm so glad you're here; let's do this!

reflection questions

1   Define your why for engaging with this book. What drew you to
    this text and what are you hoping to gain by reading it?

    _____

    _____

    _____

    _____

    _____

    _____

    _____

2   How do you personally distinguish between *teaching* and
    coaching? Consider how these concepts are similar and also how
    they're different for you.

    _____

    _____

    _____

    _____

    _____

    _____

    _____

3   As you read about what's included in this book, what part feels
    the most essential to you in this moment? Why?

    _____

    _____

    _____

    _____

    _____

    _____

    _____

notes

1

A Portrait of You, an Instructional Coach

When I transitioned from the role of a classroom teacher to instructional coach, I was both excited and intimidated. I felt excited to step into a new position and yet intimidated because I didn't yet know who I was in this new world of leadership. It took me years to pinpoint the leader I wanted to be; this chapter is about helping you do the same. In subsequent chapters we'll consider how we can best serve *others*, but we need to start here, with *you*, first. Think of this as your invitation to devote some time and reflection space to *yourself*. Whether you're new to the position or have been serving in this role for years, it's important to pause and (re-)establish your foundation so that you can better serve others.

Here, you'll identify the qualities that you most admire in other leaders, highlight and appreciate the unique gifts that you bring to this role, identify your greater why, and explore how you can live by your values in order to inspire those around you.

Leadership Traits

I get so giddy when I have the opportunity to work with instructional coaches. Here's why: they're always fantastic workshop participants. They're wicked smart, they're open to exploring new strategies and ideas, they ask super thoughtful questions, and they radiate passion and warmth. They're my kind of people. I often wonder if coaches had all of these fantastic traits before they become coaches or if these traits are the result of becoming a coach. I suppose it's one of those chicken-or-egg things: a bit of both.

The instructional coaches who truly shine are *transformational* leaders. Historian and leadership expert James McGregor Burns (1979) first introduced the concept of transformational leadership, claiming that the best leaders are those who inspire others. Transformational leaders are emotionally intelligent, full of energy and enthusiasm, and are passionate about helping every member of the group find success (Cherry, 2020). To do this, transformational leaders work to garner trust, respect, and even admiration from others—all traits that are essential for developing effective coaching relationships (Choi, 2016). Results from a study published in the *Journal of Occupational and Environmental Medicine* even indicate that transformational leaders have a positive impact on the *well-being* of their employees (Jacobs et al., 2013).

What Leadership Means to You

To be certain, transitioning from the role of a teacher to the role of an instructional coach isn't always easy and doesn't typically come with a guidebook. It's one thing to be good with students, but it's a totally different thing to be good with adults (imagine calling your colleagues' parents when they're not following the rules). As an instructional coach, you've been granted that important but daunting title of *leader*. Don't back down from this. Instead, I want you to own it. I want you to settle into it; feel it in your bones. I want you to step into your role and your title by deciding, first and foremost, who *you* are as a leader. *You* get to define what leadership means and looks like to you. This is your role to take on, and while the job description may have many bulleted points that serve as a starting place, it's the deeper definition we're looking for right now. See page 27 for the Defining Leadership organizer to help you get started in your thinking. Once you've completed that, come back here for the next steps.

Now that you've worked through the Defining Leadership organizer, I invite you to take some time to compare the two lists that it asks you to make: (1) the traits that you admire in others and (2) the traits that you personally bring to the table. Where is there overlap? Do you see any patterns emerge? For example, do you tend to admire the charisma and energy of those you admire and also recognize that you, too, possess these traits? Or perhaps you admire the confidence level of nearly everyone on your list. Take some time to journal here about what you notice about others and yourself.

_____

_____

_____

_____

_____

_____

_____

_____

_____

_____

_____

_____

_____

Now, identify any qualities that you admire in others that you'd like to emulate and add to your own list. For example, perhaps you admire your Aunt Tracy's ability to prioritize her own health by finding time to exercise every day even with the demands required of her as a business executive and would like to up your game in this area. This is your opportunity to take your leadership role to the next level. How can you build on the base that you've already established (the two lists you just made) *and* move toward becoming the leader that you truly want to be? Now's your chance: *you* get to decide who you will be as a leader in your building or district. Don't be cavalier about this; this is your legacy you're creating. Make it amazing. Spend some time reflecting on the traits that you'd like to acquire in the following space.

Establish Your Leadership Goals

Yay! Identifying and thinking about traits to emulate is a powerful step in your journey. But we're not done yet. Now that you've identified the leadership traits that you both currently possess and those that you desire to have, it's time to get down to business and make a plan as to how you're going to become *that* leader. If SMART goals (that is, goals that are strategic and specific, measurable, attainable, results oriented, and time bound, as defined by education coaches Anne Conzemius and Jan O'Neill [2014]) work for you, get after it. If SMART goals overwhelm you, find a different way. Do a quick web search and you'll find that there are CLEAR (collaborative, limited, emotional, appreciable, and refinable) goals (Kreek, 2020) and FAST (frequently discussed, ambitious, specific, and transparent) goals (Banks, 2019), HARD (heartfelt, animated, required, and difficult) goals (Murphy, 2017), and, of course, goals that you just write down on a sticky note and commit to. You do you. The main idea here is that you need to create a road map that gets you from where you currently are to where you ultimately want to be—starting now. Think of this as *self*-coaching. Just as you work with teachers to guide them from where they currently are to where they want to be, you're doing the same for yourself here.

Let's continue with our example about how we want to be like Aunt Tracy, who prioritizes her own health needs by going for a run every morning, even with a demanding career. If she can do it, you can do it, right? Consider your current state and what your own exercise and health needs are. Ask yourself some reflection questions such as the following: Do you want to run like Aunt Tracy does or do you prefer a different type of exercise? How big of a stretch will it be to actually get up and exercise every morning? Does the thought of setting your alarm an hour earlier make you want to give up? These are all important questions for consideration because if you aren't a morning person or maybe you haven't engaged in a dedicated exercise routine since college—all of which is perfectly fine—it might be too big of a jump to commit to waking up at 5:00 a.m. to go running every morning.

Perhaps, instead, you could start this week by determining what *your* needs and goals are in terms of your own health. Maybe running isn't your thing but walking is. Maybe you used to love to ride your bike but haven't been out for a spin in years. Start small. In other words, don't commit to walking and biking every day next week for an hour. Nope, that's a set up for a disaster and disappointment. Instead, how about you commit to setting the alarm fifteen minutes earlier tomorrow, laying your clothes out the night before, and going for a simple ten-minute walk around your neighborhood at least three times next week? At the end of the week, check in and see how it went, how you feel, and what you might be able to commit to next week. Perhaps you can increase your walks to every day, or maybe you decide to get up thirty minutes earlier, or maybe you want to swap your morning walk for an afternoon bike ride and see how that feels.

By using this approach now, you'll be able to call on this same process not only for your own professional goals, but you'll also have this personal experience that will assist you in helping others work towards their own goals. You're learning the important lesson of how to start small and continually check in with yourself in order to make adjustments along the way. This is exactly what author James Clear (2018) recommends in his book *Atomic Habits*. He advocates for tiny improvements that lead to big changes when done consistently over time: "You don't need to be twice as good to get twice the results. You just need to be slightly better" (Clear, n.d.a). The possibilities are endless, and only you can decide what feels right for you at this exact moment in time. Plan with grace and set realistic expectations for yourself.

You can start planning and brainstorming in the following space. Consider the leader that you truly want to be. Make a commitment. Write it down.

_____

_____

_____

_____

_____

_____

_____

_____

_____

_____

_____

_____

_____

_____

Well done! You've got a plan now for moving forward as a leader, and having a plan *always* feels good. Boom.

Identify Your Why

As we continue to paint that portrait of you as an instructional coach, let's move on to your why. Your why is your purpose, your guiding light; it's what keeps you going. For example, my why is this: *I am an author and educational consultant because inspired educators inspire students and inspired students change the world for the better.* When you know your why, or feel a sense of purpose in your life, you're better able to handle stress and regulate your emotions (Hill, Sin, Turiano, Burrow, & Almeida, 2018). I believe that it is absolutely *vital* to know your why and to keep that why in the forefront of your mind because this is one of the essential ways you can avoid burnout.

Having worked with and coached educators for over two decades, I've discovered that when educators lose their why, they succumb to the challenges of the job in a way that those who are still inspired and who are still connected to their why don't. I totally understand how it happens; it happened to me, too. I forgot my why and got so overwhelmed by the stress and demands of the job that I almost left the field completely. You've probably been there yourself; it's natural and normal to get close to complete burnout at various stages of a career in education. The challenges that we face are no joke and seem to be compounding, not at all lessening, as the years go on. When we're stressed out and exhausted and have forgotten why we chose this profession in the first place, we've got all of the essential ingredients for burnout. If, however, we're stressed out and exhausted but are still deeply connected to our why, we're better able to shut out some of the noise and keep going, knowing that we have choices and can take back some control over what's stressing us out and exhausting us.

You're still here. And that's a gift. We can't lose you. Let's engage in an exercise that will help us to reunite with our deepest why. I will give you some space to work, but first, here's an example; this is how I did the exercise and landed on the why that I shared at the opening of this chapter.

I am an author and educational consultant.

This role is important to me because I get to coach others.

This role is important to me because I get to learn from others and share that knowledge across the various places that I work.

This role is important to me because I am passionate about my work.

This role is important to me because I am making a difference.

This role is important to me because I want to help ease the burden for educators.

This role is important to me because it matters.

This role is important to me because I get to inspire others.

This role is important to me because inspired educators inspire students.

This role is important to me because inspired educators inspire students, and inspired students change the world.

With that last sentence, I knew I had it. I felt it in my body. My why: *I am an author and educational consultant because inspired educators inspire students, and inspired students change the world for the better.*

Full stop. There it is. That's it; that's my greater why. That's what I put on sticky notes and posted all over my house and in my planner. That's my North Star.

Now it's your turn!

Try this. Start with this statement:

I am an instructional coach and leader. Now finish this sentence stem:
This role is important to me because _____

_____ .

Do it again, with another response:

This role is important to me because _____

_____ .

Keep going until you find that nugget of truth that feels *exactly* right. By asking yourself to do this again and again, you're able to drill down to the exact truth in a deeper, more profound way than by simply saying the first thing that comes to mind.

This role is important to me because _____

_____.

This role is important to me because _____

_____.

This role is important to me because _____

_____.

This role is important to me because _____

_____.

This role is important to me because _____

_____.

This role is important to me because _____

_____.

This role is important to me because _____

_____.

This role is important to me because _____

_____.

This role is important to me because _____

_____.

This role is important to me because _____

_____.

When you find that *exact* truth, record it here. You'll know when you've hit on your exact truth because you'll have a reaction. When I found my true why, I felt it in my gut, and I literally let go of the pen I was writing with.

That's your greater why. Hold onto it. Do what I did, and write your why on multiple sticky notes. Post them all over your house, your office, your car, and on your bathroom mirror so that you walk with purpose into your why every single day. I've now also started writing my why in my journal as part of my morning routine to keep my purpose in the forefront of my mind at all times; perhaps you can do the same.

Identify Your Values

In her book *Dare to Lead*, Brown (2018) provides the following definition for *value*: "A *value* is a way of being or believing that we hold most important" (p. 186). When we identify our values—and then live our lives accordingly—we walk our talk (lead by example), which is an essential trait of leadership. The next exercise for you to explore as you continue to sink deeper into understanding who you are as a coach and a leader is identifying your own essential values: in other words, let's get clear on what you care about *the most* so that your leadership is congruent with your values. This next exercise will act as a way to make your true why even more powerful.

To begin, explore the list of values in figure 1.1.

Your mission is to identify the *two* that are the most important to you. That's right, *just two*. I know this is a challenge. I struggled with this myself. I started by circling *all* that felt important to me and then I kept whittling down and whittling down some more until I finally landed on my top two. (You might take a break and go for a walk here or allow yourself to take multiple days engaging in this process. There's no need to rush this.) And before you ask, Brown (2018) reminds us, "We have only one set of values" (p. 187). What you value professionally will also be what you value personally. She goes on to say, "We are called to live in a way that is aligned with what we hold most important regardless of the setting or situation" (Brown, 2018, p. 187). Your values are what will help you navigate your choices and will support your greater why as you fulfill your purpose for your work as an instructional leader.

Accountability	Fun	Personal fulfillment
Achievement	Future generations	Power
Adaptability	Generosity	Pride
Adventure	Giving back	Recognition
Altruism	Grace	Reliability
Ambition	Gratitude	Resourcefulness
Authenticity	Growth	Respect
Balance	Harmony	Responsibility
Beauty	Health	Risk taking
Being the best	Home	Safety
Belonging	Honesty	Security
Career	Hope	Self-discipline
Caring	Humility	Self-expression
Collaboration	Humor	Self-respect
Commitment	Inclusion	Serenity
Community	Independence	Service
Compassion	Initiative	Simplicity
Competence	Integrity	Spirituality
Confidence	Intuition	Sportsmanship
Connection	Job security	Stewardship
Contentment	Joy	Success
Contribution	Justice	Teamwork
Cooperation	Kindness	Thrift
Courage	Knowledge	Time
Creativity	Leadership	Tradition
Curiosity	Learning	Travel
Dignity	Legacy	Trust
Diversity	Leisure	Truth
Environment	Love	Understanding
Efficiency	Loyalty	Uniqueness
Equality	Making a difference	Usefulness
Ethics	Nature	Vision
Excellence	Openness	Vulnerability
Fairness	Optimism	Wealth
Faith	Order	Well-being
Family	Parenting	Wholeheartedness
Financial stability	Patience	Wisdom
Forgiveness	Patriotism	Write your own:
Freedom	Peace	
Friendship	Perseverance	

Source: Brown, 2018; Clear, n.d.c; Jeffrey, n.d.

Figure 1.1: List of values.

Be careful that you're not choosing values that you feel like you *should* choose but instead are identifying the traits that truly feel the most true for you. There is no right or wrong here. Some values are not better than other values.

Brown (2018) offers the following questions to help guide you as you're thinking about your choices.

- Does this define me?
- Is this who I am at my best?
- Is this a filter that I use to make hard decisions?

When you're ready, record your *two* most essential values here.

1. _____

2. _____

Now that you've identified your core values, Brown (2018) encourages us to identify three behaviors that support each value, identify three slippery-slope behaviors (behaviors that tend to lead to undesired or undesirable actions) that are outside each value, and provide an example of a time when you were fully living this value.

My two most essential values are integrity and well-being. Here's how I responded to those prompts for each of those values.

Value 1: Integrity

What are three behaviors that support your value?

1. Choosing what's right over what's easy
2. Being the same person in all situations, with all people
3. Walking my talk and leading by example

What are three slippery-slope behaviors that are outside your value?

1. Pleasing others instead of doing what's right for me
2. Pretending to like or not like certain things when I'm with different people

3. Conducting a workshop on health and wellness and then feeling shame when I celebrate with french fries after I'm done

What's an example of a time when you were fully living this value?

Just yesterday I said no to an invitation rather than saying yes out of obligation or a desire to please this person. It wasn't easy to say no, but it was what I needed to do for me, so it was the right choice. I had no regrets the following day. This is integrity.

Value 2: Well-being

What are three behaviors that support your value?

1. Abstaining from the food and beverages that don't make me feel good
2. Prioritizing my sleep and exercise or movement
3. Taking care of my mental health

What are three slippery-slope behaviors that are outside your value?

1. Drinking too much caffeine or alcohol
2. Binge-watching TV or Netflix
3. Not setting healthy boundaries around my need to be alone in order to refuel my energy

What's an example of a time when you were fully living this value?

I lived this value during the quarantine of 2020, when we were forced to stay at home for months. I chose foods that made me feel good, increased my exercise, and committed to reading more books than watching shows. I thought a lot about who I wanted to be on the other side of this crisis and made choices accordingly. Staying true to my own well-being was my top commitment during those difficult months.

Thinking through your values takes a lot of mental work. Take a deep breath, and do the same.

Record your top two values here.

Value 1: _____

What are three behaviors that support your value?

1. _____

2. _____

3. _____

What are three slippery-slope behaviors that are outside your value?

1. _____

2. _____

3. _____

What's an example of a time when you were fully living this value?

_____

_____

_____

_____

Value 2: _____

What are three behaviors that support your value?

1. _____

2. _____

3. _____

What are three slippery-slope behaviors that are outside your value?

1. _____

2. _____

3. _____

What's an example of a time when you were fully living this value?

_____

_____

_____

Finally, take some time to answer the following reflection questions regarding your values now that you have a clear vision of what they mean to you (Brown, 2018).

1. Who is someone who knows your values and supports your efforts to live them?

   _____

   _____

   _____

   _____

2. What does support from this person look like?

   _____

   _____

   _____

   _____

3. What can you do as an act of self-compassion to support yourself in the hard work of living your values?

   _____

   _____

   _____

   _____

4. What are the early warning signs that you're living outside your values?

   _____

   _____

   _____

   _____

5. What does it feel like when you're living your values?

   _____

   _____

   _____

   _____

6. How does living your two key values shape the way you give and receive feedback?

_____

_____

_____

Now, take a(nother!) deep breath and recognize all of the hard work you've just done. You've just engaged in radical reflection and deep thinking in order to not only paint the most beautiful portrait of yourself as an instructional coach, but to step fully into that vision. When we know and live by our values, we are stronger leaders. By holding true to my core values of integrity and well-being, I am a stronger leader because I have a North Star to guide my work. If I'm faced with a tough decision, I ask myself which choice supports my core values more. For example, if I get a request to speak at a conference that excites me but is in a city that's far away from where I live, I pause to consider my choices and which choice helps me stay aligned with my values. Sometimes I politely decline because my travel schedule around the time of the conference is intense and I need to prioritize my well-being. Other times, I say yes because the conference is completely in line with my mission and I have the time available to be away from home without feeling too burned out. My values help me keep my boundaries, and this makes me a stronger leader.

Now you are clear on the leadership qualities that you bring to the table and also actively working toward pushing yourself to continue on the journey that you've started here. You've also identified your greater why and backed up that vision with the two most essential values that you will lead from. This journey will in turn make you a stronger coach because you're now standing on really solid ground. You know who you are, you're connected to your purpose, and you're able to recognize when you're getting off course (your slippery-slope behaviors).

I hope you start to walk a bit taller now and feel like you're standing on solid ground as a leader in your school or district. Own your greatness. Live those values out loud and without apology. _You are amazing._ I'm so proud of you.

reflection questions

1 What did you learn about yourself through the exercises in this chapter?

_____

_____

_____

_____

_____

_____

_____

2 How will you keep what you learned about yourself in the forefront of your mind?

_____

_____

_____

_____

_____

_____

_____

3 Who can you share your work from this chapter with? How might this person help support you?

_____

_____

_____

_____

_____

_____

_____

notes

Defining Leadership

First, identify the leaders that you personally look up to. Don't limit your thinking in any way. Leaders can be fellow coaches, administrators, teachers, former bosses, public figures, your mom, or your cousin once removed—no matter what job they hold or if they have a formal job at all. A leader can be someone you know intimately or someone who you've only admired from afar (see my examples in the introduction [page 1]). Remember, a leader isn't defined by a title. Dictionary.com provides the following simple definition for leader: *a person who guides or directs a group* (Leadership, n.d.). Notice that the definition doesn't include words like *appointed* or *elected*. *Anyone* can be a leader.

Record their names here. (You can record more names in the margins or a notebook if you need more space.)

- _____
- _____
- _____
- _____
- _____

Once you've identified the leaders in your own life, begin reflecting on the qualities and traits that the people you admire possess. What is it about these people that appeals to you? Is it their positive outlook? Is it their ability to remain calm in a crisis? Is it their work ethic? Their professionalism? Their energy? Their ability to take care of themselves while also taking care of others? Get specific. Allow yourself time to ponder this so you can dig deep. Write down your observations here.

- Leader's name: _____
  - Desirable traits: _____

- Leader's name: _____
  - Desirable traits: _____

- Leader's name: _____
  - Desirable traits: _____

- Leader's name: _____
  - Desirable traits: _____

page 1 of 2

🖊 Leader's name: _____

   ○ Desirable traits: _____

Now, take some time to reflect on *your* very best leadership qualities. Do not skip this. And please don't hold back here. This is important. What is *your* it factor? In other words, what makes you unique and special? What sets you apart and makes you a leader? When others think of you and the qualities and traits that they admire, what do you think is on that list? This may take some time. Allow yourself space to ponder this. Walk away from this exercise as needed (I mean this quite literally, in fact, as I find that I tend to do my best thinking while I'm out on a walk), and then come back when you're ready. Now, write your identified qualities down. If you get stuck, ask your squad (your friends, family members, or colleagues whom you trust) to help. Hear their responses with openness (and don't you dare discredit their observations; you *are* amazing!).

My best leadership qualities:

🖊 _____

🖊 _____

🖊 _____

🖊 _____

🖊 _____

🖊 _____

🖊 _____

🖊 _____

Take a moment to reread that list and revel in the goodness of who you are. Those are your incredible and unique gifts that you bring to the people you serve. Feel proud of those traits; you've worked hard to earn them. In fact, I suggest that you keep this list somewhere safe so you can return to it on tough days or times when your self-esteem has taken a hit so you can remember who you are and what makes you such a formidable leader.

2

An Effective
Coaching Relationship

Now that we've established solid footing for you to stand on, we turn our attention toward working with others. At its core, coaching is all about relationships. And like any relationship, we start by building trust with our teachers. Then, we continually work to strengthen that relationship so that we're standing on solid ground when we begin to nudge and push our teachers to engage in the hard work of increasing their own expertise in order to positively impact student achievement.

In his foundational book *The Speed of Trust: The One Thing That Changes Everything*, Stephen M. R. Covey (2006) proposes that removing trust from any relationship will destroy it, but when trust is developed and leveraged, it has the power to help create success in every aspect of life. As you work to build trust with your teachers, focus on these essential cornerstone traits: asking good questions, listening like heaven, providing wait time, paraphrasing, and empathizing.

This chapter explores the idea of building trust with teachers and establishes these three cornerstone traits that are necessary for connection and rapport within any coaching relationship.

Ask Good Questions

Learning how to ask thoughtful, rich, open-ended questions is a skill that all coaches and teachers must master. Instructional coaching expert Jim Knight (2016) reminds us, "Dialogue is not likely going to occur unless we ask effective questions" (p. 92). When we don't take the time to plan for meaningful questions, we're thrust into throwing out simple, common, closed questions, and thus our conversations get stuck in a pattern such as the following.

> *Coach:* How are things going?
>
> *Teacher:* Fine. Things are fine. Busy, but OK.
>
> *Coach:* Anything I can help with?
>
> *Teacher:* No. I just need time to work.
>
> *Coach:* You'll let me know if I can help with anything?
>
> *Teacher:* You bet. Gotta go—I'm swamped!

Ugh. Been there, done that; as a coach, I left interactions like these feeling deflated because our conversation didn't go anywhere, and I wasn't able to help. It was only after I learned the art of questioning, which I outline in this section, that I started to steer my coaching conversations in a different, more fulfilling direction.

So how do we learn the art of asking good questions? We have to work at it. Litigators, journalists, and doctors are all taught the art of questioning, but we don't typically get this type of training as we move into our coaching roles. In an article from the *Harvard Business Review*, authors Alison Wood Brooks and Leslie K. John (2018) remind us, "Questioning is a uniquely powerful tool for unlocking value in organizations: it spurs learning and the exchange of ideas, it fuels innovation and performance improvement, it builds rapport and trust among team members." Brooks and John (2018) go on to offer the following suggestions for learning the art of asking good questions.

- Ask lots of questions, focusing on follow-up questions that keep the conversation flowing rather than choppy, unrelated questions that end up feeling more like a job interview.

🖋 Focus on open-ended questions (*why, what if, how*), as closed questions (those generating *yes* or *no* responses) can feel like an interrogation.

🖋 Start with less sensitive questions and slowly build up to questions that require more vulnerability; this builds trust. For example, begin your conversation with typical questions related to family or current events before jumping into questions regarding professional challenges.

🖋 Be conscious of your tone. You might even record yourself so that you can reflect on your tone later. Consider taking it one step further and ask someone to listen to that recording to provide you with additional feedback to reflect on. Does your tone sound inviting or irritated? Rushed or calm?

Knight (2016) offers the following additional suggestions when it comes to the art of questioning.

🖋 **Be genuinely curious:** If you enter into a coaching conversation legitimately curious to know more about the person you're coaching, you'll naturally ask better questions. As Knight (2016) says, "Curiosity is the embodiment of the principle of reciprocity. When we view conversations as reciprocal, we enter into conversations as learners instead of talkers" (p. 93).

🖋 **Be nonjudgmental:** Knight (2016) reminds us that people need to feel safe in order to engage in meaningful conversation. Safety stems from trust and allows us to share deeper emotions and to be more vulnerable with one another. In order to accomplish this, we must do the following.

  ○ Listen without assumptions and without prejudging the person you're coaching. Again, being genuinely curious is a huge help here. Enter into every coaching conversation with a desire to learn *more* about the person you're coaching rather than getting too caught up in accomplishing a task.

o Let go of the desire to give advice. Let me say that again, louder, for the people in the back: *let go of the desire to give advice.* As teachers and caretakers, we want to help and so often we offer our unsolicited advice as a way to "help," but advice giving can shut a conversation down—quickly. It's important for us to learn how to simply listen. Which brings us to listening like heaven, our next cornerstone trait.

An additional tool to keep in your back pocket is the AWE strategy (the AWE question; Stanier, 2016), which is an acronym for three magic words that can keep the conversation going: *And what else?* If you feel like teachers have more to say or are still working through an issue or a concern, simply asking, "And what else?" can help to keep them going and digging deeper.

Brainstorm some conversation-starting questions here that you could then build on to get to more serious topics.

_____

_____

_____

_____

_____

_____

_____

_____

_____

_____

_____

_____

_____

_____

_____

Listen Like Heaven

Once we ask our questions, we engage in the art of *incredible* listening. I've taken to calling the coaching dynamic I describe in this section *listening like heaven*. I'm referring to heaven here as a superlative—the best. You might say a piece of chocolate tastes like heaven. Going on vacation is heaven. Sleeping in on a Saturday and then enjoying coffee without interruption? Heaven. Listening can be like that—like heaven. To me, listening like heaven means that you're providing the gift of full presence to someone else. You're all in. In his book *The Culture Code: The Secrets of Highly Successful Groups,* Daniel Coyle (2018) beautifully describes this type of listening: "I kept seeing the same expression on the faces of listeners. The only sound they made was a steady stream of affirmations," (p. 75). You're not listening while also responding to a text message. You're not nodding but looking at something going on somewhere else. You're not half-listening, more focused on what you're going to say next. You're also not interrupting. Coyle (2018) also states, "It's important to not interrupt. Interruptions shatter the smooth interactions at the core of belonging" (p. 75). Listening like heaven, as part of a quality conversation, means that you're leaning in close, putting the phone away, maintaining eye contact, holding your tongue, resisting the sometimes over-whelming urge to butt in and interrupt, and engaging in that beautiful dance between listening and paraphrasing, listening and paraphrasing. This is next-level active listening. This builds trust, it builds connection, and it is an essential element of any quality relationship. I agree with executive coach Christian van Nieuwerburgh, who says, "Coaching is often creating a quiet space for the other person to think" (as cited in Kelly, 2019).

Successful coaching stands on the shoulders of a successful relationship, and a successful relationship depends on the ability to engage in a quality conversation that goes beyond simply posing a series of questions (even really good questions). Because we lead such immensely busy lives and have such easy access to technology and written communication, the gift of a beautiful face-to-face *conversation* is becoming a lost art in some ways. We really felt this when COVID halted our ability to be together physically.

Learning how to stay connected via Zoom or Google Meet was a new skill for many, and while it definitely feels different to talk through a screen, it's still possible to listen like heaven; it's about the time and attention you devote to the conversation, not so much the medium. Listening like this is an important part of establishing a sense of belonging.

Consider your own personal relationships for a moment. Upon reflection, do you feel like your strongest relationships are built on rich conversations? I suspect the answer to that is a clear *yes*. Think about the last time you sat down with someone you care about—either virtually or together in person—without a buzzing phone vying for your attention, without distraction—and really listened to one another. That was a gift, wasn't it? Perhaps time slowed down. Maybe you forgot about your to-do list for a moment. It may have been that you were able to sleep more soundly that night having had the opportunity to process your own thinking with a thoughtful partner. When we listen well and when we are listened to, we are connected and connection is essential to any relationship, especially our coaching relationships.

Over the years, I've identified what I believe are the next two *most* essential elements of a quality conversation: (1) providing wait (or think) time and (2) paraphrasing.

Provide Wait Time

Education researcher Mary Budd Rowe (1972) first introduced us to the concept of wait time in the classroom when she discovered the following benefits that occur when teachers wait for three or more seconds after posing a question to the class, and that research continues to be validated (McCarthy, 2018).

- The number of "I don't know" responses decreases.
- The length of answers and the correctness of answers increases.
- More students are willing to answer a question.

In coaching conversations, the idea of wait time is slightly different than in a classroom setting, and yet the benefits are similar. Consider that in a typical back-and-forth conversation each person's turn to speak lasts for around two seconds and the gap between the next person's words is just two hundred milliseconds (Yong, 2016). But when we're able to hold our tongue and pause longer than two hundred milliseconds, the length and depth of our partner's response increases, they're less likely to simply shrug their shoulders, and they're often more willing to answer a question. When we hold space for the person we're connecting with by listening fully rather than listening with the goal of responding, it feels different. Novelist Chuck Palahniuk (1999) famously writes, "The only reason why we ask other people how their weekend was is so we can tell them about our own weekend" (p. 87). Coaches must resist this impulse; it's not about us. It's a subtle but essential shift. And it's a challenging one, as it might lead to awkward silence at times, but it's vital to sit in that space because magic awaits just on the other side of those cringy moments. Like in the classroom, I've found that wait time certainly allows for a richer conversation.

One way to address the notion of awkward silence is to be up front and open about it. I will often say something along these lines when I'm coaching someone:

> Because I know how powerful wait time is, I'm working hard to lean into it in my conversations. For us, this means that I'm going to allow you to fully finish a thought before I jump in—which means that there might be a few moments of that dreaded awkward silence that we usually work so hard to fill. I don't want to make our conversation weird in any way, I just want to provide you the gift of being able to fully think through your thoughts without interruption by me. Please don't feel like you need to fill that space—I promise to not let the awkwardness go on too long.

And then we try it. And we giggle the first few times there's silence, but we keep going, and it gets easier and easier and the conversation goes deeper and deeper. It's a beautiful dance.

Paraphrase

Next, when the speaker is done talking and there's been a few seconds of silence (longer than two hundred milliseconds) to signal this, it's essential to paraphrase what you just heard *before* you offer any type of suggestion or feedback. Here are some simple suggestions for quality sentence stems for paraphrasing.

- "Let me try to capture what you just shared . . ."
- "In other words . . ."
- "It sounds like . . ."
- "There are a few different important points here, such as . . . . From what I can tell, you're mostly concerned with . . ."
- "Here's what I think you just said; please tell me if this is correct . . ."
- "It sounds like you're feeling . . ."
- "You're suggesting that . . ."
- "Let me make sure that I'm understanding what you're saying . . ."
- "Tell me if this feels right . . ."

Many of us cringe when we hear the often overused phrase, "What I hear you saying is . . ." and thus we get turned off to the idea of paraphrasing, but I'm begging you to stick with me on this. Because here's the deal: we might be *wrong* in our understanding of what our partner is saying and thus we lead the conversation down an entirely different road than the speaker intended. I can't tell you how many times I've listened to a teacher describe something to me, and after paraphrasing what I heard, he or she says back to me something like, "Well, no, that's not exactly it," and then they go on from there. It's not that I'm actually wrong in my listening and paraphrasing, it's that my teachers might still be trying to sort through the issue or concern in their own minds, and hearing me summarize their thinking thus far is helping them to narrow in on the *exact* issue or concern. And thus, we stay focused on *them*. We stay on *their* road. We don't drag them down a different path that isn't theirs. It's magic. Paraphrasing expresses empathy (which we'll explore further in the next section). When we are able to reflect people's meaning back to them, they feel truly heard (Seehausen, Kazzer, Bajbouj, & Prehn, 2012).

As an added benefit to us, paraphrasing removes the pressure of having to think of the exact right thing to say. There's no stress over fixing anything when we're engaged in this type of dialogue. I'm telling you, so many of my best conversations, coaching or otherwise, have been when I've been able to really sit with someone and simply listen and paraphrase, listen and paraphrase. In the end, I didn't provide much advice or direction; instead, I allowed my partners to find and follow their own paths while I simply gave the gift of holding space for them (by being fully present). Likewise, *I've* felt the most heard and seen when someone has sat with me and allowed me to talk my way to my own next step or solution. It feels so great to have the agency to direct your own next move simply by having time with a trusted friend or colleague who thoughtfully provides the space for you to get there on your own. As a bonus strategy, you can also tack on, "And what else . . ." (the AWE question; Stanier, 2016), the same strategy from the previous section.

Take some time to journal about a recent coaching conversation you had with a teacher and how you could have used paraphrasing as part of that conversation.

Another idea is to record an upcoming conversation so you can listen to it again in order to practice where and how you could insert paraphrasing. With practice, paraphrasing will become second nature, and those you coach will benefit.

Empathize

The final cornerstone for building trust in your coaching conversations is learning how to empathize. *Empathy* is "the ability to share and understand the emotions of others" (Molenberghs, 2020). It's important because it allows us to feel compassion for and relate to others (Damasio, 1995). It's also something that we can continually work to improve. Mohammadreza Hojat, a doctor who developed a scale to measure empathy, calls it a cognitive attribute that people can choose to develop (Boodman, 2015). When we engage in conversation with new people, walk in someone else's shoes for a while (by visiting a new neighborhood or church, or shadowing someone who has a different job than we do), read fiction or memoirs about people who are different from us, or volunteer, we are partaking in strategies that can help us increase our empathy (Miller, n.d.).

During my student teaching experience, I spent time shadowing students, and it proved to be one of the most profound lessons of that entire semester. By following one student for an entire school day, I was reminded of what it's like to be a student, and I recognized things that made me feel greater empathy for seventh and eighth graders: things like how students often get very little physical movement within the school day and that switching from mathematics to art to English in a matter of hours is mentally exhausting. I was also reminded that the teacher truly sets the tone for the class within the first thirty seconds of the period, and that the rules and expectations vary greatly from class to class and teacher to teacher. It can be challenging to keep it all straight.

This shadowing exercise instilled a deep and lasting empathy for students that impacted my entire teaching career. Thus, I recommend that coaches spend time shadowing their teachers. I recognize that coaches were once teachers, but the truth is, we only know our own experience. The act of stepping back into the world of the teachers you serve will show them that you honor and respect them and that you're there to learn and understand. For example, if you were a fifth-grade mathematics teacher, it's important to shadow teachers whose jobs look different than what you know, like the physical education teacher or the kindergarten teacher, for an entire day. Doing so will help you recognize the intense demands and pressures that these individuals feel on a daily basis. You'll have a better understanding why perhaps they don't contribute much during faculty meetings after school once you've seen that they maybe haven't had a break from students or even time to use the restroom in five hours.

Do this every year. Do this as often as you can. Tell teachers what you're doing. Explain that you're not there to evaluate or critique, instead, you're there to get a glimpse into their daily lives, to feel what it feels like to be them. Let them know that you're open to hearing them share what's hard about their day, what they're the most proud of, and what exhausts them. Share your (only kind) observations through an empathy lens using sentence starters like, "I'm in awe of how you . . .," "I never knew . . .," "I'm so glad I was able to see you . . .," or "I'll forever remember how you . . . ."

When you observe a teacher, make notes here about what you observe and what you want to remember as you coach this teacher (and others). Be sure to highlight what you want to share with the teacher as well.

_____

_____

_____

_____

_____

Before you enter into any coaching conversation, take a moment to get your head into an empathy mindset. Consider what the day or week has been like for this teacher, remember the demands and burdens that this teacher might be carrying (especially now that you've witnessed it firsthand through your shadowing experience), and set aside any judgment that may be creeping in. When we *really* understand our colleagues and when we are truly curious about the challenges they face, we start to empathize with them in more profound ways. This act of seeking first to understand goes a long way in building trust with your teachers.

An Invitation

Here's an invitation for you to play with this week. Purposefully practice the essential cornerstones that I have outlined in this chapter, both with your loved ones and with fellow instructional coaches who may also be working on building their expertise. Ask for ten minutes of time (most people are willing to give you ten minutes, especially if you honor that and don't take more) and practice the strategies outlined in this chapter.

Who you'll be speaking with: _____

Circle which skills you want to specifically practice during this conversation: asking good questions, listening like heaven, providing wait time, paraphrasing, or empathy.

Brainstorm some questions to get the conversation going (consider what you'd genuinely like to know about this person; remember to ease in and then build up to more vulnerable questions).

_____

_____

_____

_____

Consider recording the conversation (either audio only or with video) so that you can review it again for reflection purposes.

After the conversation, reflect on how it went, what you learned, how you showed empathy, and what you want to remember or try next time.

_____

_____

_____

_____

reflection questions

1   Of the essential components outlined in this chapter (asking good questions, listening like heaven, providing wait time, paraphrasing, and empathizing), where do you feel like you excel? How do you know?

_____

_____

_____

_____

_____

_____

_____

2   Of the essential components outlined in this chapter, where do you feel like you need additional practice? How do you know?

_____

_____

_____

_____

_____

_____

_____

3   Think of people you know who are good models for each of these components. How can you tap into their skills to improve your own?

_____

_____

_____

_____

_____

_____

notes

3

The Phases of the School Year and the Four Types of Support

Now that you have a better idea of your purpose and values and have established the foundational traits for coaching as well as the conversational skills that are essential for developing quality relationships, it's time to move into the *how* of the work.

This chapter will help you offer intentional and targeted coaching by matching your support to the exact needs of your teachers. We'll discuss the phases of the school year, the different types of support, and how to determine what phase a teacher is currently in. You'll also learn how to differentiate support for new teachers, teachers who are new to the building but have previous experience, and experienced teachers.

The Phases of the School Year

Many of us are familiar with new teacher mentor Ellen Moir's (2011) pivotal research around the phases of first-year teachers' attitudes toward teaching (often lovingly referred to as the *dip chart* because of the shape formed by a graph representing these attitudes; this is also how I'll refer to it from here on out).

Moir (2011) lays out six distinct phases of the school year and how new teachers tend to feel during each of these phases. In order to offer intentional, targeted, and differentiated coaching, I propose that we match our support to the phase that the entire staff or the individual teacher is currently experiencing. From my work with thousands of educators with varying degrees of experience—from newbies to veterans—I strongly believe that these phases are not unique to new teachers. I posit that experienced teachers also go through these highs and lows throughout the school year. The difference is that when new teachers hit a new phase, they don't know any different and thus believe that this phase is how they will feel forever, which is especially challenging when sliding into the dips. When experienced teachers reach each phase, particularly the challenging ones, they still feel the stress and frustration, but part of their mind gently reminds them, "Ah yes, I know what this is. This is how I feel *every* November. This too shall pass." Moir (2011) outlines the phases and associates them with the months of the school year; I've added an additional phase based on my work with educators across the United States, as noted in figure 3.1.

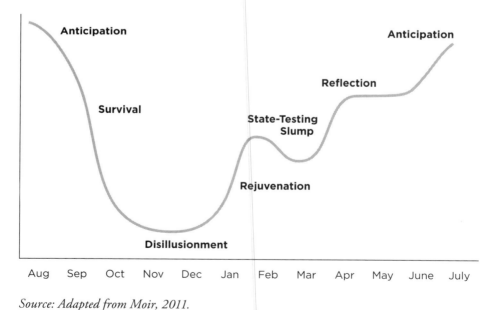

Source: Adapted from Moir, 2011.

Figure 3.1: Phases of new and experienced teachers' attitudes toward teaching.

✑ **The anticipation phase (August–September):** This is when we're getting ready to start a new school year. We're fired up and excited, we're getting our classrooms set up, and we're starting to establish systems and build relationships with both our colleagues and our students.

  ○ If we were to create a playlist for the school year, the corresponding song for this phase might be "I'm So Excited" (Pointer, Pointer, Pointer, & Lawrence, 1982) by the Pointer Sisters or "Let's Get It Started" (Adams et al., 2003) by the Black Eyed Peas. Putting a playlist together on an online music service like Spotify (http://spotify.com) might be a fun way to work through the phases with teachers; you can even invite them to add their own songs.

✑ **The survival phase (late September to October):** Here, we're starting to become overwhelmed. The stress of the job is hitting us, and we're starting to feel like ducks: appearing calm on the outside but scrambling beneath the surface. Our self-care habits may start to slip as we're getting less sleep and finding less time for exercise and meal planning, and the first round of fall sickness hits our buildings and classrooms.

  ○ The corresponding song for this phase might be "Jesus, Take the Wheel" (James, Lindsey, & Sampson, 2005) by Carrie Underwood or even "Highway to Hell" (Young, Young, & Scott, 1979) by AC/DC.

✑ **The disillusionment phase (late October to December):** This is *the* most challenging phase of the school year. We are drowning. We're deeply struggling and feel as though we're just barely hanging on by our fingernails. Our self-care is minimal, and we're questioning if we can even show up for work tomorrow.

  ○ The corresponding song for this phase might be "Take This Job and Shove It" (Coe, 1977) by Johnny Paycheck or "The End" (Morrison, Manzarek, Krieger, & Densmore, 1967) by the Doors.

- ✍ **The rejuvenation phase (January to April):** We're out of the slump or dip, and we're grooving now. We feel like we've got our feet back on the ground, and we're recommitted to the calling. Relationships are strong, students are making progress, and we have a clear vision of where we are and where we're heading. We've got this.

  - ○ The corresponding song for this phase might be "I Got You (I Feel Good)" by James Brown (1965) or "Good Feeling" (Dillard et al., 2012) by Flo Rida.

- ✍ **The state-testing slump (late February or early March to April):** This is my own personal addition to Moir's (2011) foundational work. I believe that there's a second dip that typically occurs in the spring when schools are faced with state testing, fewer breaks after spring break, and new or heightened behavior issues from students begin to rise as the weather starts to change. I don't believe this dip is as low as the disillusionment phase dip because the end of the year is around the corner, but I believe it is significant and should be addressed.

  - ○ The corresponding song for this phase might be "Yesterday" (Lennon & McCartney, 1965) by the Beatles or "Don't Stop Believin'" (Cain, Perry, & Schon, 1981) by Journey.

- ✍ **The reflection phase (April to May or June):** Here, we begin to reflect on the school year and consider what we'd like to change for next year. This phase is marked by rituals, ceremonies, and celebrations and is a meaningful time of year for staff and students.

  - ○ The corresponding song for this phase might be "Glory Days" by Bruce Springsteen (1984) or "Just Breathe" (Vedder, 2009) by Pearl Jam.

- ✍ **The second anticipation phase (summer):** Education is one of the few professions where we are granted a fresh start every single year. During the time between one school year and the next, we're able to experience that *anticipation* once again—this time for the well-deserved break that marks summer vacation.

○ The corresponding song for this phase might be "School's Out" (Cooper, Bruce, Buxton, Dunaway, & Smith, 1972) by Alice Cooper or "Happy" by Pharrell Williams (2014).

Consider how essential it is to be aware of what phase a teacher is in so that you as a coach can provide support that feels meaningful and relevant. For example, if a teacher is in the throes of disillusionment, this probably isn't the best time to analyze data with a fine-tooth comb. Similarly, if a teacher is feeling rejuvenated, it's the perfect time to engage in deep instructional coaching conversations in order to increase his or her expertise with the use of various research-based instructional strategies. While the months are a general rule of thumb, it's important to remember that not everyone hits each phase at the same time. Many teachers—particularly new educators—hit disillusionment well before October and may feel like they're still in it beyond January. Similarly, I know many teachers who feel like they cycle through each phase multiple times per year. I've even had teachers jokingly say to me, "Tina, this is the outline of my day. I wake up in anticipation, by third period I'm in survival, I'm looking for a new job at lunch, my fifth period pulls me back into rejuvenation, and I hit the pillow at night reminding myself that tomorrow is a new day." It's so true, isn't it? Even for *you,* as a coach or leader. When you reflect on these phases, I'm willing to bet that you feel each of them in your own way, too.

I show these phases and the dip chart during nearly every professional development session that I conduct, whether I'm working with newbies, veterans, or leaders, because there's a sense of relief in the recognition that we're not alone in our feelings and experiences. Even during the COVID-19 pandemic when the school year felt anything but normal, we recognized ourselves in the various phases and were able to make connections to how we were feeling based on what was happening in the world. We're reminded that *everyone* goes through these phases and has moments where we wonder if we're going to be able to get out

ed for work the next day. It's *normal*. I remember when my
ntor first showed me this chart as a new teacher who was in the
ʌ, low dip of disillusionment and thinking, "Oh, thank God.
's not just me. It can't be just me; they made a *chart* for goodness
ake. I'm not alone." And one thing we all want to feel is *not alone*.
The good news is, there are a ton of tools that we can offer to
our teachers (and use ourselves) to help us navigate each of these
phases, which I will discuss in the following pages.

The Four Types of Support

Once we understand the phases, we can consider accordingly
how to match the four types of support that we can offer to teachers. Education consultants Laura Lipton and Bruce Wellman
(2017) assert that new teachers primarily need four types of support: (1) physical support, (2) institutional support, (3) emotional
support, and (4) instructional support. I've expanded their theory
and propose that we can build on these four types of support for
all teachers—not *just* our newest educators, but also teachers who
are new to a building but have previous experience and experienced teachers, too.

1. **Physical support:** This type of support is practical
   and tangible. It includes navigating the building,
   gathering resources and materials, and specifically
   preparing for the start of the school year. This type of
   support is vital for new teachers.

2. **Institutional support:** This support involves
   understanding the culture of a building, establishing
   systems of support, collaborating with colleagues,
   and keeping up with education research. This type of
   support is essential for new teachers and those who
   are new to the building but have previous experience.

3. **Emotional support:** This type of support is
   especially essential when teachers are struggling,
   feeling inadequate, questioning their abilities,
   wearing out, and asking themselves, "Can I do this?"
   This type of support is essential for new teachers
   who find themselves in the disillusionment phase for

the first time. Here, I also include my addition of educator self-care and wellness, which are essential supports for all educators, all year long. By engaging in purposeful self-care, educators can minimize the impact of their struggle on students.

4. **Instructional support:** This is the type of support that is the most directly correlated with student achievement, as it involves helping a teacher increase their expertise with the various characteristics of effective teaching. All teachers should receive this essential support throughout their entire career.

I should note that a coach does not need to be the sole provider of all four types of support. This is important, so let me state that again: one person should not be expected to provide all four types of support to every educator in the building. Instead, it is extremely valuable to consider dividing up the physical, institutional, and emotional support among an entire staff. Think about the teachers in your building who are extremely organized and have great routines and procedures—can you tap them to help your new teachers with targeted physical support? Next, consider those who fully understand the culture of the building and honor their experience by inviting them to help with institutional support. Now, identify the mama and papa bears and those who are tuned in to wellness and health among your staff, and rely on them to help with emotional support and targeting support around educator wellness. Do you have a wellness committee that can help carry the load here? If not, it might be beneficial to put one in place. School wellness committees are typically advisory groups that focus on the health and well-being of school staff, students, and families. The Alliance for a Healthier Generation (http://healthiergeneration.org) provides a plethora of resources as well as a toolkit for schools to use.

By wrapping more arms around your new teachers in particular and dividing up the heavy load of providing targeted support, you're helping to build connections among more staff members, thus creating a sense of belonging for your newbies and those who are new to your building while also not putting a tremendous burden on one or two individuals by asking them to provide *all* the support while also maintaining their regular workload.

Note that it is essential that the person providing the *instructional support* in terms of helping teachers develop their expertise (most likely you, the reader of this book) be specifically identified and trained for the role. Team or grade-level leaders and department colleagues can provide some generalized instructional support by offering to share curriculum guides and content- or grade-level-specific resources, but the person who is specifically *coaching* a teacher on his or her use of research-affirmed instructional strategies should be highly qualified to do so.

Education researchers Robert J. Marzano and Julia A. Simms (2013) explain that those who provide targeted instructional support should perform the following actions.

- Demonstrate proficiency in increasing student achievement in their own classrooms.

- Possess a vast knowledge of curriculum and instruction.

- Interact with others in a professional and courteous manner.

- Concur with the goals of the coaching program.

- Comprehend and be able to describe what effective performance looks like.

- Engage in self-reflection and continuous improvement in their own roles as coaches.

Consider, now, how the four types of support connect with the phases of the school year.

- **Anticipation phases:** In these phases, there is an emphasis on physical and institutional support (primarily for new teachers and those who are new to the building). The first anticipation phase has a clear emphasis on physical and institutional support at the building level, while the second anticipation phase loops back to institutional support but takes a broader educational perspective beyond the building level.

> ✒ **Survival, disillusionment, and state-testing slump phases:** During these phases, we promote emotional support (with an emphasis on educator wellness and self-care). By establishing healthy habits and routines here, teachers will be primed and ready to tackle intensive instructional support next.

> ✒ **Rejuvenation and reflection phases:** Here we can focus intently on instructional support (which is essential for *all* teachers).

In figure 3.2 I illustrate the ways in which the four types of support align with the dip chart.

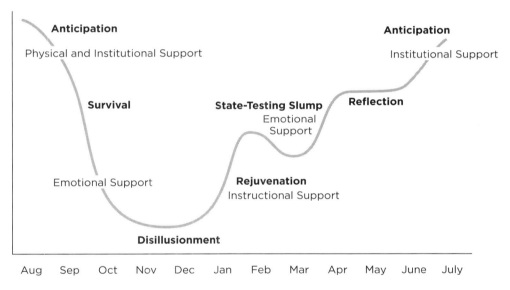

Source: Adapted from Moir, 2011.

Figure 3.2: Connecting the phases and the four types of support.

This isn't to suggest that coaches should avoid offering instructional support until February. Instead, the idea is that you *begin with* the most essential type of support—for example, emotional support when a teacher is struggling during the survival and disillusionment phases—and follow up with appropriate instructional support as needed. For example, consider a new teacher who comes to you upset and perhaps even crying and wondering if he or she is cut out to do this job. You begin with emotional support. You ask good questions, you listen like heaven, you provide wait time, and you paraphrase through an empathy lens. Once you have that teacher in a calm space and you've listened carefully in order to identify the exact problem, you can then offer instructional support that specifically addresses the concern. Often, new teachers' frustrations center around classroom management or building effective relationships with students, which are both areas where targeted instructional strategies can be extremely helpful. Additionally, emotional support could be helping the teacher get more quality sleep, helping him or her find time for mindfulness and exercise, or helping establish a morning routine that allows him or her to start the day feeling calm. When we are deliberate in the type of support that we provide, based on the phase that the teacher is in, our support becomes targeted, meaningful, timely, specific, and focused.

Determine What Phase a Teacher Is In

Usually, it's fairly easy to know what phase a teacher is in, but there are times when you might not be certain. This is especially true for new teachers who tend to put on a brave face and continually state that everything's fine when asked how things are going. When this is the case, you might ask the following questions to determine the most appropriate type of support to offer (Boogren, 2015).

- ✘ "What is your most pressing concern at this time?"
- ✘ "What do you wish you knew right now?"
- ✘ "What do you wish you had to support you?"
- ✘ "What is making your job difficult right now?"
- ✘ "What can I provide that would make your life easier right now?"
- ✘ "If you had three extra hours in the day, how would you use them?"

Take the first question, for example: "What is your most pressing concern at this time?" Consider all the various responses that you might get when posing this question.

- ✘ "I don't know how to get additional books for my next unit."

- ✎ "I'm staying at school until 7:00 each night."

- ✎ "There's an education conference that I'm interested in attending."

- ✎ "I'm scared of Billy in my second period class."

- ✎ "My lessons aren't taking as long as I planned for, and I don't know what to do with the extra ten minutes that I have."

Once you hear the response, you can begin to connect the appropriate support.

- ✎ I don't know how to get additional books for my next unit (*physical support*).

- ✎ I'm staying at school until 7:00 each night (*emotional*, *instructional*, or *institutional support*; you'll want to dig deeper to find out if this is a time management issue, a planning issue, a lack of team support issue, or something else).

- ✎ There's an education conference that I'm interested in attending (*institutional support*).

- ✎ I'm scared of Billy in my second period class (*emotional support* followed by *instructional support*).

- ✎ My lessons aren't taking as long as I planned for, and I don't know what to do with the extra ten minutes that I have (*instructional support*).

You can go about asking these questions in a variety of ways. You might send an email containing a few of these questions prior to a face-to-face meeting and ask for a quick response to help you prepare for your time together. Or you could ask these questions during a face-to-face or virtual meeting and respond on the spot. A quick survey or Google Form might also help you gather information that will reveal what phase a teacher is in.

As the landscape of education continues to evolve, we can hold onto the phases and the types of support as our sustaining pillars. Teachers will continue to experience the phases each year, with some years being more challenging or more rewarding than others, and we can modify the strategies related to each of the four types of support as we continue to evolve and grow.

reflection questions

1   Consider how you've experienced the phases of the school year personally throughout your career as an educator. How does this knowledge help you in supporting others?

_____

_____

_____

_____

_____

_____

2   How do you currently provide the four types of support? Where are you strong and where could you add support? Who might be able to help you provide each type of support?

_____

_____

_____

_____

_____

_____

3   How do you currently differentiate support for your new teachers, teachers who are new to the building but have previous experience, and experienced teachers? Did this chapter help inspire you to make changes in this area? In what ways?

_____

_____

_____

_____

_____

notes

4

Physical and Institutional Support for New and New-to-the-Building Teachers

Prior to the start of the school year and as the new year gets underway, you'll be focusing heavily on supporting your new educators, both those who are just entering the profession and those who come to you with previous experience but are new to the building. Above all else, your mission should be to create a sense of belonging for your newbies. According to psychologist Abraham Maslow (1969), after our physiological and safety needs are met, we seek to fulfill our social needs through a sense of belonging. In fact, being excluded activates the same area of our brain where we feel actual physical pain (Hills, 2018). Just like we want each of our students to feel connected and welcome, we should also strive for the same with our staff.

As you consider how to create this sense of belonging, start by designing a plan that begins immediately after hiring and centers around interactions that contribute to a sense of community within your building. In the book *Motivating and Inspiring Students: Strategies to Awaken the Learner*, Robert J. Marzano, Darrel Scott, Ming Lee Newcomb, and I (2017) address four topics related to belonging for students. In this chapter, I propose planning your physical and institutional support around the same four areas for our newest educators in order to ensure a sense of belonging: (1) inclusion, (2) respect, (3) affection, and (4) cooperation.

Physical support includes practical, tangible help that involves materials and logistical issues. It includes everything from helping new teachers secure supplies to getting classrooms set up for the first day. *Institutional support* includes helping new teachers understand school processes and developing school culture and working to develop lifelong learners who seek continuous improvement. Both of these supports, physical and institutional, are associated with the anticipation phase, as they ensure a successful start to the year. When we intentionally run our physical and institutional support strategies through the filter of ensuring a sense of belonging, we're working to establish a culture that retains new teachers. In fact, a study from the Learning Policy Institute shows that when new teachers receive mentoring and extra resources, first-year turnover is cut by more than half (Sutcher, Darling-Hammond, & Carver-Thomas, 2016). Later in the chapter, I will also discuss the unique challenges of handling teachers who are hired after the school year has already begun.

Inclusion

You want to make your new hires feel included as quickly as possible. The foundational invitational education framework (Purkey & Novak, 1996, 2015) can be a helpful tool for this. Originally designed for teachers to consider the needs of their students, coaches can tweak this framework to consider the needs of their new and new-to-the-building educators. The invitational education framework has two dimensions: (1) invitation and (2) intention. For our work, *invitation* refers to how our support contributes to or takes away from a sense of inclusion. *Intention* refers to how a coach actively creates and reflects on these aspects for his or her new staff members. In other words, coaches should strive to create support that is *intentionally inviting*, particularly for their newest educators.

Consider the following sample *physical* and *institutional* su
strategies that would be *intentionally inviting* prior to the st
the school year.

- A snail-mail postcard of congratulations upon hiri

- A personal welcoming phone call

- A one-to-one, in-person meeting (at a coffee shop or your own home) to get to know one another

- An email or hard copy of essential information regarding things like when and how to access the classroom and building keys, important dates (such as new teacher orientation), contract information, and so on

- Welcome traditions (West-Rosenthal, 2017)
  - A welcome breakfast, brunch, or lunch
  - School spirit gift bag (include essential supply items like pencils, sanitizing wipes, and dry erase markers, as well as a staff T-shirt, stuffed mascot, or something similar)

- Other strategies you have:
  - _____
  - _____
  - _____

Most schools host a new teacher orientation prior to the start of the school year. This ranges from one day to multiple days and is an important time to help set your new teachers up for success. However, it's imperative that we don't overwhelm our new teachers with too much information here. Often this is the very first day on the job, so nerves are high and new teachers' brains are hijacked by trying to determine where to sit and how to ask questions, trying to remember names and faces, and so on—similar to how students feel on the first day of school. Think back to your own new teacher orientation; were you relaxed and able to retain all the essential information that was provided to you or were you like me, a bundle of nerves, barely able to remember my own name?

It's important to strike a balance between what is *essential* to present on this day and what can wait or can be included in a digital or print resource that new teachers can access later. Also remember that teachers "who showed higher levels of stress at the beginning of the year displayed fewer effective teaching strategies over the rest of the school year . . . than did the teachers with lower initial stress levels" (Sparks, 2017). Consider how you want your new teachers to *feel* at the end of the day and plan accordingly. For example, you might want your teachers to feel safe, welcomed, excited, and ready. Now consider how you can tailor your time to address each of these core desired feelings and outcomes.

It's also important to consider differentiating the day for those who are new to the building and those who are new to the profession. It is a good idea to have both groups together for certain portions of the day but then divide them up as needed for other times of the day. A good starting place is to create a list of the physical and institutional support needs for each group so you can decide when they should be together and what to address when they're in separate groups. The following list includes some examples to get your thinking started. The strategies marked with an asterisk are those most likely to be essential for teachers both new to the profession and new to the building, and that you could therefore offer to the full group in the morning. You could then provide the remaining strategies to the teachers who are new to the profession while the experienced teachers have time in their classrooms (or engage in another meaningful experience).

- **Help arrange, organize, and decorate the classroom:** This includes procuring desks, books, and supplies; considering the traffic flow; being mindful of safety issues; and ensuring there are no unnecessary distractions on the walls.

- **Give a tour of the building*:** This might be done via a scavenger hunt or simply as a walking tour. It's helpful to provide a map with teachers' names and subject areas or grade levels. Bonus points if you can also include photographs so teachers can start to put names with faces.

- ✍ **Help prepare for or script the first day of school:** It can be especially beneficial to help new teachers write a script for the first day (or even the first few days) to help ease nerves and ensure that they are establishing strong relationships with students from day one.

- ✍ **Explain administrative procedures*:** This includes everything from taking attendance and collecting forms or dues to creating a system for make-up work and students who are absent to emergency procedures, and much more. It's helpful to have these essential procedures in writing so new staff can access them as needed.

- ✍ **Demonstrate how to use school technology tools*:** This might include the gradebook, computer log-in information, copiers, learning management systems, student technology tools, and so on. Also be sure to cover the school technology guidelines for both students and staff and who to contact for tech support.

- ✍ **Create emergency substitute teacher plans:** Most schools require all teachers to have a set of lesson plans that can be used in times of emergency to cover their classes. They typically include things like class rosters, seating charts, the daily schedule, classroom rules and procedures, and hall passes or other essential forms. It's especially helpful to have a template to start with, outlining the essential components that new teachers should include. Having examples from experienced teachers can be helpful as well.

- ✍ **Explain the procedure for securing a substitute teacher*:** How do you secure a sub? How do you request someone specific? Is there a list of reputable subs for the school or district? How far in advance should you submit your request? What happens if no sub is available?

- ✍ **Help prepare for students with unique needs:** Ensure that the new teacher understands the needs of his or her students, including those with an individualized education program (IEP) and other support plans. Acronyms can be overwhelming, so be sure to thoroughly explain each designation and provide a key.

Establish classroom rules and procedures: New teachers may need help establishing their personal rules and procedures. Ensure they are coming up with a reasonable number of rules and that their rules mirror the schoolwide expectations. Help teachers plan how they will communicate the rules to students (and families) and what the consequences will be when the rules aren't followed.

- **Help launch initial communication with parents:** New teachers can feel intimidated when they reach out to parents and guardians. It's helpful to work with new teachers to establish a communication plan, especially for those who teach elementary-aged students. Again, tap into veteran staff to help share their plans and offer templates to new teachers.

- **Explain the school mission and vision*:** Explicitly share the mission and the vision of the school and the district and provide background as to how these came to be. Help new teachers understand the core beliefs of the school in relation to the following essential questions (Muhammad, 2011).

  ○ What is the purpose of our school?

  ○ Who are our students?

  ○ What are their strengths and needs?

  ○ How can our collective efforts improve the quality of their education and the quality of their lives?

  ○ What are we collectively willing to commit to and sacrifice?

  ○ What specific indicators of progress will we track to ensure we are making progress in meeting the needs of our students?

- **Establish a support network*:** Help teachers connect with staff via their collaborative grade-level or content-area teams. Schools that function as PLCs should have robust team frameworks in place. Ensure that experienced staff members have a plan to welcome new members to their teams, and help new teachers understand the dynamics of the communities they will be involved with.

- **Explain the teacher evaluation process*:** A general overview is helpful even though the details can wait until the school year gets underway.

- **Establish collaboration time with appropriate colleagues*:** Help ensure that new staff members know how to connect with their paraprofessionals, special education colleagues, response to intervention staff, counselors, speech pathologists, psychologists, and so on.

- **Foster relationships with coworkers*:** Ensure that new teachers are included in staff activities like sports leagues, happy hours, book clubs, trivia nights, and so on.

- **Facilitate involvement with extracurricular activities as desired*:** Share opportunities to be involved with students outside of the classroom, including coaching or sponsoring sports teams, clubs, and so on. Be cautious of putting too much responsibility on new-to-the-profession teachers, however.

- **Add your own ideas here:**

Respect

In order to ensure that your new educators feel a sense of belonging, make sure that you offer respect. Respect involves not only taking your teachers' thoughts, feelings, and ideas seriously but also respecting their *time*. Your goal is for your new teachers to feel respected by the experienced staff and for your experienced staff to also feel respected by your new teachers without overwhelming them. To do this, consider the following *institutional* support strategies.

- During the first staff meeting, introduce each new staff member and highlight his or her background and unique gifts. If you plan to have new teachers introduce themselves, be sure to prepare them ahead of time and let them know exactly what you'd like them to share; perhaps have them practice with you, as this can be especially intimidating for young teachers. It's easy to forget that some teachers are extremely uncomfortable talking in front of adults, even though they're pros in front of students.

- Allow experienced staff to introduce themselves as well. If your staff is too large to do this as a whole group, consider breaking into smaller teams or groups and setting up strategies for connecting.

- If you're in charge of planning icebreaker activities, be respectful of your new teachers' comfort levels. Just as we're careful to not embarrass our students, let's also be careful not to embarrass our new staff members. Offering choices and allowing teachers to demonstrate their *strengths* is a good starting place. Quick, low-risk icebreakers include activities like the following.

  - *Two Truths and a Lie*—Everyone writes down three sentences with information about themselves, but one sentence must be a lie. Other people then ask follow-up questions to determine which statement is the lie.

- ○ *Sit Down If*—Everyone sits in a circle and one person asks a series of quick yes-or-no questions. Participants sit down if they can answer *yes*; the last person standing is proclaimed the winner.

- 🖊 Additional icebreaker examples are included later in the chapter in the Cooperation section (page 68). Add your own ideas here.

_____

_____

_____

- 🖊 Be conscious of teachers' needs in relation to time and their overwhelming, all-consuming desire to be in their classrooms getting ready for the first day of school. Carefully consider what you *must* address prior to the start of the school year and what can wait. Your teachers will be incredibly grateful for this, and it will help you develop trust and mutual respect. Put your empathizing skills to work here as you recall what it's like to be new and where you'd want to spend your time and energy.

Affection

Another way to welcome new staff and ensure that they feel connected is to show affection by demonstrating genuine care for each new teacher. Small expressions of affection can go a long way in letting new staff members know that you are fully invested in them and excited to support them. Consider the following *physical* and *institutional* support strategies connected to affection: acquiring personal information, offering simple courtesies, and using humor.

Acquire Personal Information

Gather information from your new staff members that will be helpful in offering support (particularly emotional support) throughout the year. Figure 4.1 (page 66) offers some helpful information to include.

send personal notes)

on (names, ages, relationship)

- Favorite snack or beverage

- Favorite way to relax

- Favorite book genre to read

- Favorite school supply

- Favorite song (use this to create a staff playlist that can be used during faculty meetings, professional development, and other gatherings)

- Preferred pronouns

- How the new staff member likes to be recognized or celebrated

- Other ideas:

Figure 4.1: Personal information worksheet to support new staff members.

*Visit **go.SolutionTree.com/educatorwellness** for a free reproducible version of this figure.*

Use this list throughout the year to surprise your teachers and demonstrate affection. Placing their favorite snack in their mailbox or dropping off their favorite beverage in the afternoon are simple gestures that can mean a lot.

Offer Simple Courtesies

Just as we work to connect with each and every student every day, we should also ensure that we're doing the same for our new teachers. This can be done by simply:

- Stopping in to say hello in the morning
- Congratulating small and big wins—both professionally and outside of school
- *Listening like heaven* during one-to-one conversations (see page 33)
- Asking about the weekend, family members, and so on
- Offering sincere compliments
- Smiling and using teachers' names in conversation
- Thanking new teachers for their contributions
- Other ideas:

_____

_____

_____

_____

_____

Use Humor

Ah, laughter. We feel better when we're laughing, and you can certainly use humor as a way to demonstrate affection. Research shows that people who laugh together like each other more (Suttie, 2017) and humor tends to imply a level of comfort around one another (Marzano, Scott, Boogren, & Newcomb, 2017) and increases connection (Mayo Clinic, 2019). I'm certain that many educators can recall personal experiences that remind us of the importance of laughter and humor. When I think back over my career and all the people I've worked with, I feel the most affection for those that I was able to share a laugh with.

Consider how you can incorporate humor as *institutional* support into your new teacher orientation and throughout the year by sharing funny tidbits via newsletters or email, to kick off a faculty meeting, on professional development days, and so on. For example, you could play a game where you utilize the playlist that I presented in chapter 3 (page 43) by playing the chorus of each song and asking teachers to identify the matching phase or having teachers come up with their own playlists to match the phases. Or you set up activities that make people laugh and feel good, like a staff dodgeball tournament, lip sync competition, or team talent show, as well as by simply allowing teachers to share the funniest thing they heard, said, or saw that week as an opening activity when you're all together. Additionally, you can share funny (but appropriate) memes, videos, and stories with your new teachers. Gerry Brooks (https://bit.ly/2HdjdxO) and Bored Teachers (www .boredteachers.com) are two sources of humor that many educators can relate to.

Cooperation

Finally, cooperation is a great way to create a sense of belonging for new teachers in your building. This is especially helpful before school starts, as you can create activities where experienced staff members and new teachers work together in a way that's fun and that helps establish relationships. You can do the following activities with staff members (and then use them with students, too) in order to provide *institutional support*.

- **Line-ups:** Have staff members line up based on a specific criterion, such as by years of experience, by birthday, or alphabetically by last name. You can make this more difficult by creating parameters staff must abide by, such as lining up without talking or with blindfolds on.

- **Interviews:** Pair experienced and new staff members together and invite them to conduct interviews with their partners. Each person will report out to the rest of the staff some of the highlights of the interview.

- **Bingo boards:** Create bingo boards with personal information in each box. Examples include:
  - Has a pet
  - Was born in a different state
  - Went to _____ university or college
  - Has children
  - Has never had a cavity
  - Likes chocolate
  - Loves to read
  - Plays a musical instrument
  - Played a sport in high school or college
  - Is left-handed
  - Goes by a nickname

Allow time for the staff to mingle and sign off on each other's bingo cards. Have a fun prize for the winner. You could also have your staff compete in a scavenger hunt. Goosechase (https://bit.ly/3lZewqN) provides several ideas.

Late Hires

Sometimes you hire a new staff member later in the school year. This is a tricky situation for everyone: "Teachers hired after the start of the school year are twice as likely to leave their schools—or the profession altogether—within a year" (Sparks, 2011). Teachers who start mid-year don't have the time that other teachers had to prepare; they're expected to jump in and hit the ground running. And with nearly half of all teachers considering job changes with the added stress and demands of the COVID-19 pandemic (Tate, 2020), it's hard to imagine that late hires especially won't be at a significant disadvantage. Because of this, it's even *more* essential to ensure a sense of belonging for late hires. Try to do what you did with your other new hires with these folks as well: call them to welcome them as soon as they're hired, send a congratulatory postcard or note, make sure that a welcome bag is waiting for them, and ensure that he or she has the essentials to get started: keys, supplies, access to technology, and so on. Perhaps arrange for the current sub to stay one additional day so you can have time with the new hire to make sure that he or she is ready to go, especially if the teacher is new to the profession. Be thoughtful about assigning a mentor and asking other staff members to check in on him or her and do all you can to help get this person up to speed as quickly as possible. Be sure to check in on him or her often; you might even remind yourself via your agenda, as it can be so easy for new hires to slip through the cracks with all the responsibilities of the school year.

Remember, also, that new hires may experience multiple phases at once because of the additional stress they bear. For example, they might be in the anticipation phase *and* the survival phase simultaneously when they first begin, as it's especially challenging to start teaching after the school year is already underway but also exciting to land the job. This means you'll need to tread carefully and work hard to not overwhelm new hires. Plan to present new information in chunks rather than all at once, and be conscious of what information is essential right now and what can wait until they get their feet on more solid ground. Think also about removing any extras from their plates; offering small gifts like releasing them from bus duty or covering their lunch supervision for the first few weeks can go a long way in helping out new hires. Consider how you can help new hires establish relationships with students, particularly if they're new to the profession. Remind them of the importance of establishing trust, security, and safety before moving into academics, even if it's the middle of the school year.

Providing thoughtful physical and institutional support is an essential part of retaining your newest educators and helping to create a true sense of belonging. As we'll see in the next chapter, emotional support and educator wellness are also critical factors to consider.

reflection questions

1 How do you or can you differentiate your initial support for brand-new educators versus those who are new to the building?

_____

_____

_____

_____

_____

_____

2 Review your new teacher orientation plan and consider what is essential and what might wait until a later time. How do you want your new teachers to *feel* at the end of the orientation and how can you plan the day accordingly?

_____

_____

_____

_____

_____

_____

3 Consider your experienced staff and who you might reach out to in order to learn more about their experiences as beginning teachers. Jot down what you'd like to inquire about here. Sample questions could be: How did our school create a sense of belonging when you were hired? What would have increased your sense of belonging?

_____

_____

_____

_____

_____

notes

5

Emotional Support
and Educator Wellness
for All Teachers

The demands of teaching are incredible. As any educator knows, this isn't a 9:00 to 5:00 job and we don't just simply turn it off when we walk out the school doors at the end of the day. Instead, we think about our students and our lessons all the time. We worry, we fret, we wonder, we grapple . . . and that takes a toll on us. Recognizing and working to alleviate this toll is an important part of a coach's role. This chapter addresses emotional support through the lens of educator wellness and self-care as ways for supporting the social-emotional learning needs of the adults in our schools and classrooms.

First, we'll explore the demands that teachers face, including decision fatigue, burnout, and challenges in regard to students' backgrounds, then we'll move on to how coaches can help teachers face these demands and overcome them. In chapter 1 (page 9), we discussed how important it is to take care of yourself as a coach in order to help others; now, we'll talk about how to pass that commitment to self-care on to both new and experienced teachers so they can best serve their students. This type of support is essential for the entire school year but is particularly important during the challenging survival, disillusionment, and state-testing slump phases.

The Impact of the Challenges Teachers Face

The cornerstone of effective schools, like those that are designated High Reliability Schools (Marzano Resources) and Professional Learning Communities at Work® (Solution Tree), is creating conditions where our students can be healthy, safe, engaged, and supported in their learning (Eaker & Marzano, 2020). Such conditions become an impossible aim if the adults in the building are depleted, worn out, burned out, and completely exhausted. Decision fatigue and students' challenging backgrounds and behaviors all help contribute to burnout, and all three are difficulties that teachers must reckon with.

Decision Fatigue

The average teacher makes 1,500 educational decisions every school day. This means that in an average six-hour day *in front of students* (I know teachers work way more than six hours a day altogether), teachers make more than four educational decisions per minute (Cuban, 2011; Goldberg & Houser, 2017). And that is exhausting. Plus, that number only refers to *educational* decisions; consider *all* the decisions and choices that we make during the course of a day, starting the minute the alarm goes off in the morning: *Am I getting up or hitting snooze?* (decision 1). *Do I really need to shower today, or can I sleep for a bit longer?* (decision 2). The average adult makes about 35,000 remotely conscious decisions each day (in contrast, a child makes about 3,000; Hoomans, 2015). We make 226.7 decisions each day about food alone (Hoomans, 2015)!

Consider what this means for new teachers. One of the main differences between being a novice teacher and an experienced teacher is the amount of automaticity, or unconscious competence, the experienced teacher has developed around certain tasks and procedures (Neer, 2014). For new teachers, *everything* is new and thus, *another decision.*

Of course, everyone makes decisions, especially during the workday, but the difference for us as educators is that there is a *student* who depends on us making good decisions. Our choices matter. Big time. Sure, some decisions carry more weight than others, but choices about instruction, assessment, planning, and student placement must be thoughtful decisions, requiring a clear and fresh mind. Our decisions are also relentless. We don't get to take an hour lunch off site to reset ourselves; instead, we make decisions all day long—nonstop—right through our twenty-minute lunch break. The problem should start to become clear here. Because teachers are faced with *so* many decisions and relentless choices—with little time during the day to rejuvenate or rest—our brains become tired and the consequences for this can be detrimental both for our own health and well-being, and for our students as well. When we're mentally exhausted, there's a much greater likelihood that we'll do something we regret, like losing our temper and yelling at students, ignoring those who need our help, or easing up when we should be pushing students to do their best work (Dawson, 2017). We lose, and our students lose.

Consider that your willpower is like a muscle and that like the other muscles in your body, willpower can get exhausted when you use it over and over again—such as when you're faced with a lot of decisions (Lamothe, 2019). The consequence of making those 1,500 (plus) educational decisions each day is that each choice chips away at our willpower, eventually depleting it completely. "When humans are overstressed, we become hasty or shut down altogether, and that stress plays a huge role in our behaviors," says Tonya Hansel of Tulane University (as cited in Khaer, 2020). Because the brain works like any other muscle, it gets tired just like any other muscle. For the brain, the more decisions and choices you make, the more tired it becomes. If your days are filled with heavy decisions, like most of our days are as educators, we wear our brain out to the point of decision fatigue. In the book *Willlpower: Rediscovering the Greatest Human Strength*, authors Roy Baumeister and John Tierney (2011) define decision fatigue as emotional and mental strain that results from a burden of choices. Decision fatigue has three primary impacts: (1) it reduces our ability to distinguish between positive and negative traits, (2) it causes decision avoidance, and (3) it diminishes our willpower (Barile, 2019).

When I first discovered this research, I had such an aha moment. *This explains so much.* Consider days when you're faced with relentless decisions with very little time to yourself (a lot of days, I'm assuming). Do you find yourself completely spent and unable to even expend the energy required to decide what to make for dinner by the time you get home? Do you have great intentions in the morning that you'll work out after school but then 3:30 rolls around and you couldn't possibly make that happen?

It's not your fault.

It's not that you didn't receive the magical willpower gene that your friend or sister or spouse seemed to get. It's not a defect. The truth of the matter is, you've chosen a profession where your willpower could easily be spent by 10:00 in the morning, depending on how your day is going. *Whew!*

So what happens when we've reached decision fatigue and our willpower is shot? Our brain starts looking for shortcuts (Mesh, 2018). Consider whether these feel familiar to you at all.

- **Shortcut 1:** When faced with a decision, you act impulsively, without considering the full range of consequences for your decision (for example: *Hit send on that angry email right away! What could possibly go wrong?*).

- **Shortcut 2:** You engage in the ultimate energy saver: simply do nothing (for example: *I don't feel like cooking dinner. I'm just gonna hit the drive-through.*).

Our goal is for our teachers to have the ability to make quality decisions when the high-importance, high-time tasks come up, even after a long day of teaching (more on that in a little while). We want teachers to offer the same level of focus and enthusiasm to students in their afternoon classes as their morning classes. Do you ever have important meetings after school? Don't you want your teachers to make the same high-quality decisions after school that they would make the next morning, particularly when the decisions have to do with your most vulnerable students? What if that student was your own child? *Exactly.*

Student Backgrounds and Challenging Behaviors

Up to two-thirds of students in the United States have experienced at least one type of serious trauma, including abuse, neglect, natural disaster, or witnessing violence (Minahan, 2019). Nearly 22 percent of all children have experienced two or more types of trauma (Price & Ellis, 2018). According to the Centers for Disease Control and Prevention (2020), trauma is potentially the greatest public health issue facing our students; female students and students from families with low socioeconomic status, especially students of color, are especially heavily impacted in this area. Trauma impacts students' brains and cognitive processes, making important skills like critical thinking and problem solving difficult and contributing to the likelihood of emotional outbursts (Keels, 2018).

The COVID-19 pandemic both created and added to stress for students. Many were isolated from their friends, teachers, supportive adults, teams, and were at home where they felt the financial, social, and emotional stresses that their families may have dealt with, including greater violence (Phair, 2020).

Students who experience trauma often aren't able to express their emotions in productive ways and instead demonstrate their distress through aggression, avoidance, shutting down, or other difficult behaviors (Minahan, 2019). Of course, this creates a challenging environment for teachers, particularly for teachers who are exhausted, stressed, and on the verge of burnout. It's like the perfect storm—students who are stressed in classrooms with teachers who are stressed do *not* support our goal of creating schools and classrooms where *all* students are healthy, safe, engaged, and supported in their learning. Teachers who work with students who have experienced trauma can show signs of vicarious trauma, fatigue, and burnout (Phair, 2020).

Consider some of the potential stressors that educators face as a result of working with students who have experienced trauma (Henson, 2020).

- Regularly interacting with students who exhibit challenging behaviors

- Hearing about abuse and neglect that students have experienced

- Worrying about students' safety or their future

- Feeling responsible for (or powerless) to help a student

- Trying to engage all students in distance learning

When added to an already demanding job, these stressors (and additional decisions and choices) just might be the breaking point for educators. There are four pillars for schools to focus on that balance taking care of students while also taking care of teachers (Henson, 2020).

- **Pillar 1:** Focus on educator wellness. Adults must be regulated themselves so they can help a student regulate.

- **Pillar 2:** Build strong relationships with students and families.

- **Pillar 3:** Provide predictability. Let students know what's going to happen, why, and when.

- **Pillar 4:** Teach regulation. Effective regulation includes the ability to manage one's thinking, emotional responses, attention, and physical reactions.

It can be helpful to be cognizant of these pillars when planning emotional support for your teachers that also helps students.

Burnout

Teachers who are burned out feel emotionally exhausted, begin to develop a negative attitude toward their students, parents, and colleagues, and feel a significantly reduced sense of self-esteem and accomplishment (Lynch, 2016). Additionally, teachers who reach this point are absent more, less effective in their teaching, struggle with their relationships with both students and colleagues, and are less committed to their job (Lynch, 2016). Stress, more so than low pay, is now the top reason why public school teachers quit (Will, 2021). With 93 percent of teachers reporting high stress, high burnout, and low coping skills (Riley-Missouri, 2018), we have a massive problem in our field.

Additionally, teaching during the COVID-19 pandemic added additional pressure to an already high-stress job (American Federation of Teachers, 2017; Walker, 2018). A 2021 research report from the RAND Corporation emphasizes this point with the following key findings: almost half of the teachers who voluntarily stopped teaching in public schools after March 2020 and before their scheduled retirement left because of the COVID-19 pandemic (Diliberti, Schwartz, & Grant, 2021). Teaching during the COVID-19 pandemic exacerbated stress by forcing teachers to, among other things, work longer hours and navigate an unfamiliar teaching environment, often with technical issues (Diliberti et al., 2021). One of the authors of the RAND report, Heather Schwartz, sums this up: "Stress, stress, stress—that seems at the heart of teachers' decisions to leave . . . COVID has fanned the flames of stress" (as cited in Will, 2021).

Now What? An Action Plan to Prioritize Educator Wellness

So, what does all this have to do with how you coach others? It has *everything* to do with it. We know that research-affirmed educational strategies and pedagogy are only as good as the person providing them. In other words, as coaches, we can offer someone the most amazing strategy to try in his or her classroom, but if that person is completely exhausted and wiped out by decision fatigue and other challenging factors, that strategy isn't going to have the desired effect on student achievement. Additionally, retaining our teachers matters because when we lose teachers, student achievement is negatively impacted (Diliberti et al., 2021) and one of the reasons that teachers leave our profession is stress. Thus, we must work to help our teachers conserve their brains. (Side note: this also goes for *you* and the other leaders in your building.)

What we've explored so far sounds like all bad news, and unfortunately, it is. The question now becomes, What do we *do* about it?

There is a solution to many of the challenges we face, and it rests in educators' wellness and self-care. When educators work to establish healthy habits and routines, they are better equipped to take care of their students (Boogren, 2018). Similarly, when coaches, administrators, and building and district leaders take care of themselves, they're also better able to serve their constituents and are also seen as leaders who walk their talk when they encourage self-care and wellness for their staff—I've seen this over and over again.

In my books *Take Time for You: Self-Care Action Plans for Educators* (Boogren, 2018) and *180 Days of Self-Care for Busy Educators* (Boogren, 2020), I thoroughly tackle the subject of educator wellness and self-care. Both of these books are designed to be used either individually, with accountability partners, or as an entire staff, and would be beneficial additional resources to bolster your emotional support. Additionally, I am co-director with Tim Kanold of Solution Tree's Wellness Solutions for Educators, an initiative in which we offer a comprehensive framework of support for schools and districts looking to support their educators' health and well-being in concrete and manageable ways. Here, I propose that we narrow our focus to decision fatigue and work with our teachers to ensure they have the mental capacity and energy for the important, time-consuming decisions that our classrooms require.

A huge part of this solution lies in *regulating* (scheduling decisions that are less important but will take more time), *automating* (handing off decisions that are less important and don't need as much time), and *effectuating* (just doing things that are more important and take less time) our decisions and choices (Pasricha, 2016). For example, instead of checking your phone every time you hear the notification sound, regulate your email and text habits by designating forty-five minutes in the morning and forty-five in the afternoon to read and answer all emails and texts. Or you can list non-urgent tasks that come up and do them in blocks of daily or weekly time that you set. Your goal here is to schedule windows for less important and more time-intensive items so that your mental energy isn't gradually sapped by them throughout the day. To automate your mornings, you could set a map app on your phone to determine your fastest route to work or sign up for automatic bill pay. Your goal here isn't to avoid decision making;

it's to automate decision making so you don't have to think about it over and over again.

As noted previously, some decisions aren't open for regulation or automation. These are important but less time-intensive tasks that require you to simply do it. You simply get 'er done and you move on. In other words, you *effectuate* these tasks. For example, you effectuate picking up the kids from daycare; it's not really possible to automate or regulate it, so you just do it. For some important but short-term tasks, one trick that I've found helpful is to use television personality and motivational speaker Mel Robbins's (2018) five-second rule. The five-second rule states that the second you feel an instinct, a desire, or a push to act on your commitment, you immediately start counting backward from five (5-4-3-2-1-*go!*) and you just do the thing. *Should I go fill up my water bottle? . . . Oh, but I don't feel like getting up . . . 5-4-3-2-1-go!* Stand up and do it—go fill up your water bottle and be done with it. Hydration is important, but it takes very little time. Don't overthink it.

It's important to acknowledge here that as educators, we chose to work in a profession where we *can't* regulate and automate most of our day. In fact, one of the traits of an expert teacher is the ability to make changes *in the moment* (Griffith, Bauml, & Quebec-Fuentes, 2016; Schön, 1983), thus suggesting on-the-spot decision making, and lots of it, is part of the job. What then do we do as educators? For us, it becomes essential—dare I say *mandatory*—that we regulate and automate everything we possibly can.

Before we move on, let me take a moment to clarify how our decisions relate to the tasks that we do throughout the day. Decisions represent tasks; once we decide on something, the task we need to do becomes clear. Decision making creates tasks, and if we can organize our decision making, the tasks will follow suit. Like if you decide to wear your red shirt today, your task becomes to get dressed. You always had to get dressed, but the decision was the precipitating factor that allowed you to get it done. If you waste your brain power hemming and hawing about which shirt to wear, you're already wearing yourself down; if you regulate that decision to take place the night before, you can put on the shirt in the morning without a second thought.

When we have regulated, automated, or effectuated some of our decisions, what we have left are those that are most important and will take the most time. These are the doozies. These are the *essential* decisions. These are the decisions that matter. We need our brains to be firing on all cylinders for these bad boys. Examples of these types of decisions at school include creating the bell schedule for the following year, deciding on placements for students with special needs, creating proficiency scales and common formative assessments, designing unit plans, and conferring with students. When we work to create daily habits and rituals that organize and reduce the number of decisions that we must make, we can save our willpower and help avoid decision fatigue, thus ensuring that we're better able to meet the needs of our students—and ourselves. Yay!

So let's work through how exactly we might do this (and help others do it). Start by considering some of the decisions and choices that you make on a daily basis. The running record for a typical teacher might look something like this, with asterisks to show which tasks require the most dedicated thinking.

- Hit the snooze button—yes or no?
- What am I wearing today?
- Am I going to work out after school or not?
- What do I need to pack in my gym bag?
- What am I eating for breakfast?
- What am I eating for lunch?
- What do I need to bring with me to school?
- Should I take the highway or backroads to school?
- Do I have time to stop for coffee?
- What am I doing today? Do I have all the materials?*
- How am I going to kick off the next unit with my students?*
- How am I going to structure our next unit? How will I differentiate for my second period class?*

✐ I need to set up calls with Amber's mom and Erin's dad—when will I have time for that?*

✐ Should I make copies now or wait until lunch?

You get the idea. Yes, this is daunting, and yes, this list only covers the first few hours of the day. But once we have a baseline list, we have something to work with.

To help you start to get yourself organized, try it out here in the space provided, maybe starting with one block of the day at a time. Don't overthink this; just go with your gut. Once you've worked through this process yourself, you can more easily introduce it to the teachers you work with.

○ Decision or choice: _____

○ Decision or choice: _____

○ Decision or choice: _____

○ Decision or choice: _____

○ Decision or choice: _____

○ Decision or choice: _____

○ Decision or choice: _____

○ Decision or choice: _____

○ Decision or choice: _____

○ Decision or choice: _____

○ Decision or choice: _____

From here, you can begin to think about how to organize your decisions. First, review your list and place a star next to each one that will require your best and most dedicated thinking. That leaves the remaining decisions as those in which you might be able to regulate or automate, and those that you can effectuate. What decisions represent tasks that you can block together? Which ones can wait? What can you get done now? If you can't figure out a way to regulate or automate the decision, it's probably a task that requires effectuation; you just have to do it. Don't worry about writing anything down quite yet; this is just time for you to start reflecting on your decisions and what your next step might be.

Finally, we have those items that you marked with a star, indicating decisions that are the most important and require your best and most dedicated thinking. You haven't been putting them off—you've simply done a little work to make sure you can commit to tackling them with your full mind and energy. The reward here is that if you've regulated, automated, and effectuated the other tasks, you *will* have the brain power to be thoughtful and make decisions that you not only don't regret, but are proud of. This is our goal.

Here's how our typical teacher might work through the sample list given previously.

- Hit the snooze button—yes or no? *Effectuate. Just get up!*

- What am I wearing today? *Regulate this the night before.*

- Am I going to work out after school or not? *Regulate this by scheduling workouts on my calendar.*

- What do I need to pack in my gym bag? *Regulate this by packing it the night before.*

- What am I eating for breakfast? *Automate this by having the same thing every morning.*

- What am I eating for lunch? *Automate this by having the same thing and regulate this by packing my lunch the night before.*

- What do I need to bring with me to school? *Regulate this by packing my bag the night before.*

- Should I take the highway or backroads to school? *Automate this by letting my Waze app take me to school.*

- Do I have time to stop for coffee? *Automate this by setting up my coffee maker at home the night before.*

- What am I doing today? Do I have all the materials?*

- How am I going to kick off the next unit with my students?*

- How am I going to structure our next unit? How will I differentiate for my second-period class?*

🖋 I need to set up calls with Amber's mom and Erin's dad—when will I have time for that?*

🖋 Should I make copies now or wait until lunch? *Effectuate—just get it done now.*

If you use this process with your teachers, you might ask them to first record their decisions on their own (provide them with a unit of time) and then bring those decisions to their team so that members can help one another divide up their daily tasks.

I've found it particularly useful for educators to work together to brainstorm ways to regulate, automate, and effectuate their daily decisions, enabling them to create action plans that they can use right away. For example, if a teacher is struggling with feeling disorganized during first period, she could concentrate on listing her morning decisions and her team could help her come up with ways to organize those decisions to enable her to concentrate better. See figure 5.1, page 86, for an example of what this might look like. (A reproducible template is available on page 93.)

Suggest that teachers try out their action plans for a few weeks and make adjustments as needed. Rather than automating and regulating *everything all at once*, encourage your teachers to focus on just a few things at a time. Accountability partners can be especially useful here.

If your teachers work in collaborative teams as part of a PLC (DuFour, DuFour, Eaker, Many, & Mattos, 2016), this is an excellent structure for this type of work. Teams can work together to divide and conquer tasks that can be regulated, automated, or effectuated in order to commit to being fully present and committed to the most complicated decisions and tasks they face. Similarly, grade-level or content-area teams can do this or spend time during professional development days focused on this aspect of educator wellness. For example, relying on an agenda (and sticking to it) is a way to regulate your work. Additionally, dividing and conquering tasks can be a way to effectuate, and saving challenging tasks like creating proficiency scales or designing assessments for late-start days or full professional development days rather than tackling these at the end of a long workday can be essential for your team's ability to engage fully in their best thinking.

Decision or Choice	Category (Circle one.)	What's My Plan? (How will you regulate, automate, effectuate, or dedicate brain power to this decision?)	How Is It Going? (Do you need to make any adjustments?)
Do I hit the snooze button?	Regulate Automate (Effectuate) Dedicate brain power	Just get up. NO snooze!	The 5-4-3-2-1-GO strategy works! It really works! I'm up!
What am I wearing today?	(Regulate) Automate Effectuate Dedicate brain power	Decide on and lay out my clothes the night before.	This is so helpful; I'm going to try deciding on the clothes for the entire week on Sunday so I can regulate this even more.
Am I going to work out after school?	(Regulate) Automate Effectuate Dedicate brain power	I'm scheduling my workouts on my calendar just like any other appointment: Monday, Wednesday, Friday, and Saturday; I'm also packing my gym bag the evening before.	When it's on the calendar, it gets done!
What am I eating for breakfast?	Regulate (Automate) Effectuate Dedicate brain power	I'm going to have the same breakfast every day; I don't care enough about breakfast for this to bother me. From here on out, it's a hardboiled egg and a banana. Done.	Easy-peasy; I hard boil a big batch of eggs on Sunday, so I'm set for the week.
What am I doing today? Do I have all my materials?	Regulate Automate Effectuate (Dedicate brain power)	This is something that requires dedicated brain power, so I need to make time for this. Rather than saving this for the morning, I'm going to commit to doing this before I go home each day.	It feels so much better to tackle this before I go home; I'm better able to relax in the evening and I'm not panicked on my way to school in the morning.

Source: Adapted from Pasricha, 2016.

Figure 5.1: Action plan example.

Additional Strategies for Emotional Support

Emotional support is essential all the time, but there are times when you should focus even more intently on making sure teachers are caring for their own needs. And it's also important to know other ways to make sure teachers are receiving this support.

Offer Support During the Survival, Disillusionment, and State-Testing Slump Phases

Thus far, we've discovered ways to emphasize emotional support for teachers that can, and should, occur throughout an entire school year. As noted in chapter 3 (page 43), it is also important to provide additional, targeted emotional support strategies during the difficult survival, disillusionment, and state-testing slump phases.

First off, now is the time to lean into your listening like heaven practice. Often when teachers are overwhelmed, they're not able to identify a single concern or issue. When teachers are really struggling, invite them to have a one-to-one conversation with you. Assure them that you won't take too much of their time (remember the magic of promising just ten minutes) but stress the importance of this meeting. When you're together, sit across from each other without a physical object in between the two of you if possible, make eye contact, and gently ask them to tell you what's going on. This is where you *must* listen carefully, because their thoughts will likely be scattered and jumbled. Try to pick up the core pieces, listen for patterns or similarities, and pay attention to things that they mention more than once.

When it's time, use one of your sentence starters (see chapter 2, page 29) to paraphrase the essential aspects of what they just said. Here, they may validate your assessment, or they may shake their heads and keep talking because you haven't yet found the root of the problem. That's OK. I have found that when teachers are in the depths of the dip or the slump, their thinking can be erratic and scattered, and so their description of what's going on will most likely be erratic and scattered as well. Keep doing the listening and paraphrasing dance until you're able to identify the main concerns. Next, I recommend asking teachers about their most basic physiological needs: "How are you sleeping? Are you drinking enough water? Are you eating enough? How are you moving your body?" Typically, the response to these questions isn't positive—hence, another reason why they're feeling overwhelmed. As a coach, you now get to practice offering targeted support—starting with emotional support and following up with instructional support as appropriate.

Here are several strategies that I've provided as emotional support that might be useful for you as well.

- Try to drink at least six glasses of water (or more) per day. (Start by adding just one glass per day if you aren't drinking much water to begin with.)

- Eat without distractions—allow yourself time to sit down with your meals.

- Schedule time to exercise or move your body in your calendar as you would any other appointment. Remember that this isn't selfish; it's essential.

- Keep walking shoes at school so you can take quick walking breaks throughout the day.

- Do brain-break activities alongside your students, such as simple stretches, mindful breathing, or jumping jacks.

- Set a reminder to go to bed earlier.

- Keep your electronics out of your bedroom.

- Try calming activities in the evening: reading, taking a bath, listening to quiet music, and so on.

- Stand outside in the sunshine for a few minutes each day.

Pick one of these strategies or think of your own and spend a few moments planning when and how you could incorporate it into your day.

_____

_____

_____

_____

_____

_____

_____

_____

You can then follow up with instructional support based on what you learned from listening and paraphrasing. Maybe this teacher needs support around implementing a new rule or procedure in the classroom. Perhaps there's a struggle with a particular student or an entire class and this teacher could use a strategy on building relationships. It could also be that this teacher is having trouble garnering his or her students' attention and so an engagement strategy would be particularly useful. See chapter 6 (page 95) for additional information regarding instructional support.

Look for Other Ways to Offer Emotional Support

Consider how other staff members or your wellness committee can support you here. Here are a few ideas for what you can do.

- ✎ Validate teachers' feelings and concerns by reassuring them that their feeling are normal and will not last forever.

- ✎ Send encouraging notes and messages. Periodically sending positive notes, emails, and texts can go a long way in providing emotional support.

- ✎ Celebrate success together. Keep track of teachers' successes and specific achievements and celebrate those with your teachers.

- ✎ Make time to play or create. Encourage fun activities that help to relieve stress like coloring, painting, or participating in team sports or games.

- ✎ Surprise staff by canceling a faculty meeting; encourage staff to use the extra time in a meaningful way. Invite them to document how they used their time and share those photos or videos with the staff.

- ✎ Enlist parent volunteers to help recognize staff (beyond what you already do during teacher appreciation day or week) by providing surprise treats or gift certificates to local businesses.

✍ Add your own ideas here:

_____

_____

_____

_____

_____

Educator wellness should never be an afterthought: it's an essential aspect of our role as coaches. Think of the instructions you receive when you board an airplane. The flight attendant points out that you should reach up and get your own oxygen mask in place before helping a child or other dependent. Along the same lines, encourage your teachers to secure their own oxygen masks first so they can support their students (and other staff members).

reflection questions

1   Before coaching others through the process of regulating, automating, and effectuating decisions, try it out for yourself. List your tasks and decisions, decide how to regulate, automate, and effectuate them, and then reflect on how this impacts the most complicated tasks that you're faced with. What discoveries or aha moments did you find?

_____

_____

_____

_____

_____

_____

2   How do the leaders in your school or district model educator wellness and self-care? How do they support it among staff members?

_____

_____

_____

_____

_____

_____

3   How do you take care of yourself? Reflect on how you're walking your talk when it comes to self-care and wellness. Where are your celebrations, and where might you focus your attention?

_____

_____

_____

_____

_____

_____

notes

Action Plan to Organize Daily Tasks

After creating a list of daily decisions and choices you make each day and identifying some that you can regulate, automate, effectuate, and spend your most dedicated thinking on, choose a few decisions during a time of day when you tend to feel most stressed and fill out the following action plan to help you commit to organizing your decision making.

Decision or Choice	Category (Circle one.)	What's My Plan? (How will you regulate, automate, effectuate, or dedicate brain power to this decision?)	How Is It Going? (After you try out your plan for a while, consider whether you need to make any adjustments.)
	Regulate Automate Effectuate Dedicate brain power		
	Regulate Automate Effectuate Dedicate brain power		
	Regulate Automate Effectuate Dedicate brain power		
	Regulate Automate Effectuate Dedicate brain power		
	Regulate Automate Effectuate Dedicate brain power		

Source: Adapted from Pasricha, N. (2016). The happiness equation: Want nothing + do anything = having everything. New York: Penguin.

6

Instructional Support
for All Teachers

Now that we've worked through the first three types of support, it's time to focus on instruction. Instructional support is the type of support that is the most directly correlated with student achievement, as the emphasis here is on increasing teachers' skills in the classroom. This chapter explores the ways that coaches can provide instructional support for all teachers, with the ultimate goal of increasing a teacher's expertise in the classroom in order to positively impact student achievement. While instructional support is the type of support that coaches emphasize most heavily during the rejuvenation and reflection phases of the school year, such support is relevant the entire year and should be used as backup for the other three (physical, institutional, and emotional) forms of support.

Develop Expertise

During professional development workshops with educators, I often ask participants to engage in a dialogue around whether they agree or disagree with the following statement: *effective teachers are made, not born*. This always leads to a lively discussion where we dig into identifying the traits we probably are in fact born with (an affinity for working with students and gobs of patience) and those that are developed (pretty much everything else) in order to become really good at our jobs.

We are already well aware that teaching is an incredibly nuanced and challenging profession. As former NASA scientist turned teacher Ryan Fuller (2013) puts it, "Teaching isn't rocket science. It's harder. To solve engineering problems, you use your brain. Solving classroom problems uses your whole being." The ultimate goal for instructional coaching should be to help teachers increase their expertise in order to continually improve their skills and therefore their ability to increase student achievement. Research clearly shows that student achievement is higher for students with more skilled teachers (Jackson, 2018; Marzano, Frontier, & Livingston, 2011; Opper, 2019) and thus, developing teachers' pedagogical skills should be our top priority when it comes to providing instructional support.

How, then, do we build teachers' expertise? Researchers K. Anders Ericsson, Michael J. Prietula, and Edward T. Cokely (2007) purport the following necessary ingredients.

- Engage in deliberate practice, defined as "practice that focuses on tasks beyond your current level of competence and comfort" (Ericsson et al., 2007).

- Work with a coach.

- Believe that you *can*.

You've got that second bullet point taken care of already (yay, you!) so let's focus first on exploring deliberate practice and then consider how we can increase our teachers' sense of self-efficacy (or a belief that they can indeed increase their expertise).

Deliberate Practice

Not all practice makes you perfect. Instead, you need to engage in *focused* or *deliberate* practice in order to develop expertise (Ericsson & Pool, 2016; Ericsson et al., 2007). Focused practice means pushing beyond just doing what we're already good at over and over again because if we're only practicing what we're already good at, we're not likely to make big gains in complex endeavors. As a high school tennis player, I used to love to practice by hitting the tennis ball against a wall over and over again—mostly forehand strokes. I'd practice like this for hours—mainly because I loved to do it and I was already pretty good at this skill. Unfortunately, this didn't really improve my abilities on the actual court where I needed to do a lot more than hit easy forehand strokes. If I truly wanted to increase my expertise, I needed to get focused and relentlessly spend time on the tough stuff: serves, my backhand swing, and dominating the net. Deliberate practice requires us to spend significant time working on what we *can't* do well (Cole, 2016; Ericsson & Pool, 2016).

In thinking about deliberate practice in the world of education, you might start with your new teachers and present them with real-life teaching scenarios that require action and ask them to talk through or role-play with others how to handle each of those scenarios, with detailed precision. Offer feedback regarding their choices and gentle course corrections if needed, pushing them to stick with the role-play even when they're not exactly sure what to do. By practicing what we're not already good at, we're increasing our expertise. Do this type of activity over and over and over again. Examples of situations that you can coach others to work through include disruptions, management issues, challenging student behaviors, difficult interactions with parents or guardians, technology stumbling blocks, and working through actual lessons. You might tap on your own experiences to use or invite your experienced teachers to record scenarios that you can use with your new teachers for practice.

To help experienced teachers continue to increase their expertise in a similar way, you might present atypical or rare situations that push them beyond what they've grown accustomed to on a regular basis (for example, the skilled use of technology is often a new area of opportunity for experienced teachers). Examples of these types of situations include scenarios like losing all access to technology, pivoting to distance learning and then back into face-to-face teaching, various hybrid teaching scenarios, and dealing with particularly challenging student behaviors. Make note of any out-of-the-ordinary, novel scenarios that come up during your coaching conversations with individuals so that you are continually adding to your resources here. You might also swap scenarios with your colleagues in other buildings or through your online professional learning network.

Another way to encourage deliberate practice is to ask teachers to create specific growth goals so that they can improve specific aspects of their teaching skills. When teachers write their own meaningful growth goals and create a specific plan for reaching those goals, they are setting themselves up for opportunities to engage in deliberate practice, thus working toward increasing their expertise. The key factor here is creating an environment where teachers are able to truly engage in growth goals that *matter* and around areas where they genuinely need to improve. So often, we (yes, I did this, too) choose meaningless growth goals because they're typically tied to our evaluation, and so this feels like a hoop to jump through rather than a desire to actually improve our craft. We choose goals that we're already pretty good at because we can manipulate the data and avoid the hard work that comes with focused practice. By building trust, modeling your own work around your personal growth goals (see chapter 1, page 9), engaging in deliberate practice yourself, and ensuring that school administrators aren't measuring goals punitively, we can begin to change the common and unfortunate narrative around goal setting. Ask for your administrators to support you here by allowing you to lead this work rather than making this part of the evaluation process.

Educator and blogger Jennifer Gonzalez (2014) provides five meaningful questions to help teachers uncover opportunities for *authentic* growth, and I've added one more related specifically to pedagogy (see figure 6.1).

Take a moment of quiet reflection to work through each question slowly and thoughtfully. These questions can help you uncover areas of potential growth that you can create growth goals around. With each question, take note of things that give you positive feelings, negative feeling, and mixed or unclear feelings.

1. Look around your classroom or picture it in your mind. What parts of the room make you feel tense, anxious, or exhausted? What parts make you feel calm, happy, or proud? Why?			
Positive:	Negative:		Unclear:

2. Open up your plan book or planner and start browsing. Pay attention to how you feel as your eyes meet certain events and obligations. What days and weeks give you a lift when you see them? Which ones make you feel irritated or frustrated? Why?			
Positive:	Negative:		Unclear:

3. Take a look at your student roster or class list. What do you feel when you consider each name? Which students make you feel relaxed, satisfied, and proud? Which students make you tense? Why?		
Positive:	Negative:	Unclear:

4. Mentally travel from classroom to classroom, picturing each teacher in your building. What are your feelings as you approach each one? Which coworkers give you a positive feeling, which evoke a neutral feeling, and which ones make you feel nervous, angry, or annoyed? Why?		
Positive:	Negative:	Unclear:

5. Consider these education buzzwords and how you feel about each one. You can also add your own to this list.

- Technology
- Differentiation
- Data
- Research-affirmed instructional strategies
- Professional learning communities
- Rigor
- Standards
- Distance or hybrid learning
- Assessment
- Student Engagement
- Equity
- _____
- _____

Positive:	Negative:	Unclear:

6. Consider your own pedagogy and what feels easy and what feels challenging to you this year. Consider all aspects of your teaching here, including how you provide feedback to students, your use of informal and formal assessments, content lessons, student engagement, rules and procedures, relationships, and establishing high expectations for each student. Is there an area where you'd like to experiment with new or different strategies? Do you feel stuck in a certain area? In what area can you push yourself to next-level greatness?		
Positive:	Negative:	Unclear:

Source: © Gonzalez, 2014. Adapted with permission.

Figure 6.1: Questions to stimulate authentic growth.

*Visit **go.SolutionTree.com/educatorwellness** for a free reproducible version of this figure.*

Now, having considered these questions, teachers should identify the areas that offer an opportunity for true change, or growth. These may be positives that they want to put more energy into, negatives that they want to change, or ambiguities that need more time and investigation. Ask your teachers to consider areas where they can truly engage in deliberate practice—areas where they need to grow and might feel especially challenged. Encourage them to not shy away from this challenge; remind them that this is how they increase their expertise. They can record notes for each area. From here, ask teachers to create a concrete plan to address each *priority*. Depending on the priorities and action plans that they've identified, they might want to rank order their goals so that they're not attempting to tackle too much at the same time. See figure 6.2 for an example of what this might look like.

	Priorities	Action Plan
Area 1: *Classroom*	I love where I've displayed student work. I don't have enough room to easily move around the current seating arrangement.	Add a second space for additional student work. Change the physical layout of the desks; go visit other classrooms for ideas here. Notes: *This is an easy area to work on; I'll do this immediately. I'll go visit the other teachers' classrooms on my floor for new ideas.*
Area 2: *Planning*	Wednesdays are my longest days, and I always feel exhausted and irritated by the time I get home.	Commit to taking an actual lunch break on Wednesdays where I don't meet with students and I don't attempt to multitask by working while I eat. Notes: *This is an easy area to work on; I'll implement this immediately by blocking out my calendar and letting students know that I'm unavailable on Wednesdays.*
Area 3: *Students*	I'm still struggling with my third-period class. I lose my patience so quickly with this group.	I'm going to take a restroom break between my second- and third-period classes so I can do a quick two-minute mindfulness meditation to put myself in a different headspace before I start this class. Notes: *I'm going to download two quick meditations on my phone so that I can try this tomorrow.* I'm going to set an intention to have a positive interaction with each student in this class every single day. Notes: *I'm going to add this to my journaling as part of my morning routine.*

Area 4: *Colleagues*	I'm super grateful for my grade-level team.	I'm going to share my gratitude at our next team meeting. Notes: *I'm excited to do this; it will feel so good!*
Area 5: *Professional Practice*	I need to learn more about creating quality assessments.	I'm going to bring this up with my grade-level team so we can work on this together. Notes: *I'm curious as to what my colleagues will say when I bring this up; I'm hopeful we can work on this together.* *Follow-up: Yay! My teammates also want to learn more about this, so we're going to create a plan together to tackle this.*
Area 6: *Pedagogy*	I need additional strategies related to student engagement; I'm tired of the ones I use all the time.	I'm going to identify new strategies that I can try from *The New Art and Science of Teaching* (Marzano, 2017) book that we received this year. Notes: *This is where I truly need to engage in deliberate practice. I'm going to work with my coach on this area in particular as I'm not entirely sure where to start.*

Source: Adapted from Gonzalez, 2014.

Figure 6.2: Plan template for narrowing focus.

*Visit **go.SolutionTree.com/educatorwellness** for a free reproducible version of this figure.*

Experienced teachers will most likely be able to do this exercise on their own, while your new teachers may need additional guidance or direction, perhaps from looking at samples completed by other teachers; you might even direct your new teachers to the exact area and priorities that they should start with based on what you've observed. For example, if you've noticed that one of your beginning teachers is struggling with student behavior, ask him to narrow in on area 3 only and work with him to identify priorities and create an action plan to address these concerns.

Because it's important to know what your teachers are working on so that you can support them, consider creating a master spreadsheet of all teachers' goals and priorities. You can also use this information to create cohorts of teachers who have similar goals so that they can support one another and work together on their action plans. Additionally, in schools that function as PLCs, collaborative department- and grade-level teams may choose a goal to work on together. In fact, many schools ask collaborative teams to create a team goal together and then ask individual teachers to choose their own goal, too; it's important for coaches to be aware of these so they can offer support as necessary.

Your expertise as an instructional leader will prove invaluable in helping your teachers create an action plan around their goals. Be prepared with some starting place ideas, but be open to collaborating more as a *thought-partner* (someone who challenges one's thinking and helps examine assumptions rather than taking the lead in decision making; Anderson, 2012) as your teachers create goals and develop action plans that truly feel meaningful to them. This in turn helps them develop their self-efficacy, which we discuss more in the next section.

Increase Self-Efficacy

Teacher self-efficacy means that teachers believe that what they do makes a positive difference for their students. Clearly, it is essential to have this belief when engaging in deliberate practice because, as we've learned, this type of practice requires us to spend time engaged in something that we're not currently good at and that can be challenging. It can be tempting to keep doing what we're currently doing and getting frustrated about things that aren't going well, without taking the necessary steps to make changes in our approaches and practices. I know I did this at times when I was still in the classroom. I'd recognize that the negative behavior of some of my students was escalating and my frustration was increasing but all I really did was complain about it to my colleagues and yell louder at my students rather than reflecting on the root cause of the behavior and new strategies that I could try. Four strategies that you can offer teachers to help face these challenges in a more constructive way are (1) development scales, (2) video reflection, (3) collaboration, and (4) collective efficacy.

Developmental Scales

To help your teachers develop a sense of efficacy, you can use a reflection scale that supports teacher development and is connected to pedagogy. By using a scale that emphasizes growth, teachers can determine where they currently are and where they want to be with opportunities to celebrate improvement along the way, thus increasing a sense of efficacy (Lopez-Garrido, 2020). If you begin with a general scale, you can make adaptations for any strategy or behavior related to pedagogy (area 6 from figure 6.2, page 101) that a teacher is currently deliberately practicing and help that teacher increase expertise and tap into self-efficacy. In *Becoming a Reflective Teacher* (Marzano, 2012), a book to which I contributed, we provided a scale for teachers to use for conducting a self-audit in terms of their competence in relation to the elements of Marzano's powerful instructional framework, which outlines the components of great teaching. Robert J. Marzano, Cameron L. Rains, and Philip B. Warrick (2020) update the scale in *Improving Teacher Development and Evaluation* (see figure 6.3).

4 Innovating	3 Applying	2 Developing	1 Beginning	0 Not Using
In addition to level 3 (applying) performance, the teacher identifies students who do not exhibit the desired effects related to this element. The teacher adapts behaviors and creates new strategies for their unique needs and situations.	The teacher engages in behaviors related to this element without significant errors or omissions, and a majority of his or her students exhibit the desired behaviors and understandings related to the element.	The teacher engages in behaviors related to this element without significant errors or omissions, and understands important information related to this element.	The teacher engages in behaviors related to this element, but with significant errors or omissions.	The teacher does not engage in behaviors related to this element.

Source: Adapted from Marzano et al., 2020.

Figure 6.3: Self-reflection scale.

This scale is incredibly helpful in that it is useful for both self-reflection *and* feedback. Personally, in coaching, I suggest removing the numbers from the scale, simply because, like grades, the number ends up trumping the descriptions and this scale is about *increasing expertise,* not assigning a measurement score. Additionally, when there are numbers attached to the rubric, our brain starts attaching those levels to evaluation and this rubric is *not* about evaluation. Instead, the purpose of this tool is to encourage teachers' own self-reflection and coaching conversations focused on teacher growth. Coaches are not evaluators, and coaching isn't the same as evaluating, and so this scale is not about evaluating a teacher; instead, it's about developing expertise and tracking progress. To match the purpose of this text, I offer a modified scale in figure 6.4, with a slight variation of the language and the removal of the numbers.

Innovating (I)	Applying (A)	Developing (D)	Beginning (B)	Not Using (NU)
I differentiate the instructional strategy or behavior in order to reach each learner. *There is teacher and individual student evidence here.*	I monitor and adjust the strategy based on the impact it is having on student outcomes. *There is teacher and student evidence here.*	I use the strategy or behavior but do not have fluency with it yet. *There is more teacher evidence here.*	I am just starting to utilize the strategy or behavior and so it's not quite right yet. *There is some teacher evidence here.*	I have not tried the strategy or behavior yet. *There is no teacher evidence here.*

Figure 6.4: Progress-tracking scale.

In this version of the scale, Not Using is the starting place; the teacher has learned about a new strategy or behavior but has not tried it yet, so there is no teacher evidence of the strategy at this point. For example, a teacher is interested in using the four-corners strategy as a way to incorporate more physical movement into her classroom but has never tried it. Here, the coach might outline the steps of the strategy for the teacher.

As the teacher is trying the strategy or behavior out for the first time, she is at the Beginning level on the scale and is likely not using it well just yet, but so far there is evidence that the teacher is at least attempting the strategy. Perhaps she presents the four options and asks students to move to the corner that represents their choice, but she neglects to provide directions about what students should do once they've moved to their corners.

After more time and reflection on the strategy on her own and with her coach, the teacher moves to the Developing level. Here, the focus is on the mechanics of the strategy or behavior itself— when and how to do each part, timing, common questions, stumbling blocks, and so on. There is additional teacher evidence building at this level. Now, the teacher in our example knows to provide oral and written directions about what students will do once they're in their chosen corners.

In order to move to the Applying level, which is the goal level for proficiency with a strategy, the teacher now has enough experience with the strategy or behavior that he or she can spend less time focusing on the logistics of the strategy itself and more time considering how the strategy or behavior impacts student learning. Additionally, at this level, teachers are able to make needed adjustments based on how students respond to the strategy or behavior. At the Applying level, there is both teacher and student evidence that the strategy is working or having the desired effect. Now, the teacher in our example is able to *monitor* how the four-corners strategy is going. She moves from corner to corner, listening in to students' conversations, and when she recognizes that one corner has more than ten students and only one person is sharing, she quickly responds by breaking the group into three smaller groups so students can converse with one another more easily.

Finally, as teachers discover tweaks and various ways to use the strategy or behavior, through self-reflection and continued work with a coach, they can increase expertise and move to the Innovating level as that knowledge becomes the basis for differentiation and meeting the needs of each and every learner in the classroom. Here we see teacher evidence and individual student evidence. The teacher in our example recognizes that a few students seem to struggle with this activity because they simply go where their friends are. In response to this, and after discussing options with her coach, the teacher pauses to have these students record which corner they're going to go to and why before they actually stand up and move.

This scale becomes the foundation for tracking progress toward increasing expertise and self-efficacy by providing actionable feedback on a teacher's performance. Each step is an opportunity for reflection and dialogue between you as the coach and the teacher that you're working with. Talking through the levels of the scale becomes the basis of your feedback whether you're working with new teachers or experienced teachers. For new teachers, you'll spend more time coaching from the Not Using level through the first few levels, while experienced teachers will more often be at the Developing or Applying levels, working toward Innovating.

As part of your dialogue and feedback, you'll help your teachers to flesh out what the strategy or behavior is (the teacher evidence) as well as the intended outcomes for students (the student evidence), based on their chosen pedagogy-related growth goals. Again, new teachers will need a lot of support and guidance here, and experienced teachers will be able to flesh out each level alongside you. Note that we start our scale at the highest level of the rubric because we read from left to right and want teachers to start with the end in mind. If you're used to seeing scales start at the lowest level and build up, feel free to adjust this scale, too.

Figure 6.5 presents a fleshed-out example of the scale, which the teacher from our example might have used with her coach.

Innovating (I)	Applying (A)	Developing (D)	Beginning (B)	Not Using (NU)
I am focused on how the four-corners strategy helps individual students pay attention and stay focused on the lesson and am able to make adjustments in the moment.	I am focused on how the four-corners strategy helps students pay attention and stay focused on the lesson and am able to make adjustments for the whole class in the moment.	After reflecting on the four-corners strategy, I've made changes and am trying those changes in my classroom.	I am attempting the four-corners strategy as a way to incorporate physical movement into my classroom for the first time.	I have not tried to incorporate physical movement into my classroom yet.

Figure 6.5: Progress-tracking scale for the four-corners strategy.

Tracking progress as a teacher moves from one level to the next is the next essential component of building instructional knowledge and skills *and* is a way to provide actionable feedback on a teacher's performance. A simple tracking guide, such as the one in figure 6.6, which has been adapted and modified from Marzano and colleagues (2020), can serve as an essential coaching tool.

To use this chart, teachers record their growth goal, their initial rating, their desired rating, and attach a date to their goal if appropriate. Every time teachers engage in deliberate practice related to their growth goal, they record the date and place a dot or checkmark in the box that represents where they feel they are in relation to the scale. There's also room at the bottom of the form to add reflections in the form of key learnings and new questions. This also serves as a guide for coaching conversations, as you can offer additional feedback based on their own reflections

Progress-Tracking Guide

Name: *Melissa Langer*

My growth goal:
Increasing student engagement by utilizing the four-corners strategy

My initial level (circle one): (NU,) B, D, A, I

My goal is to reach level (circle one): B, D, (A,) I

My goal is to reach this level by: *By the time I finish this unit*

I will engage in deliberate practice in the following ways (you can continue to add to this as you work through the strategy and reflect on your progress).

- *Use the four-corners activity to discuss our story*
- *Assign a character from the story to each corner of the room*
- *Ask students to decide which character is the most important in the story and move to the corner that represents their choice*
- *Once in the corner, they will work with their group members to identify three reasons that support their choice*
- *Students should be in groups that are no larger than five; if there are more students than that in one corner, I'll divide the group up accordingly*
- *Students will determine which corner they're going to move to and why before moving so that they don't simply follow their friends.*

Whenever you engage in deliberate practice related to your goal, place a mark and record the date in the following scale.

Innovating (I)					
Applying (A)					x
Developing (D)				x	
Beginning (B)		x	x		
Not Using (NU)	x				
	Date: *Sept. 9*	Date: *Sept. 12*	Date: *Sept. 12*	Date: *Sept. 12*	Date: *Sept. 20*

Key learning and new questions:

Oral directions aren't enough; I need to provide written directions at each corner.

When there's more than five students in a group, not everyone participates—I'll need to break larger groups into smaller groups.

Some students seem to simply move to the corner where their friends are rather than making an informed decision—I need ideas for how to handle this from my coach.

Thanks to my coach, I had students record their choices and why before moving and checked in with Eric and Brian before I asked students to move, and that helped a ton.

Source: Adapted from Marzano et al., 2020.

Figure 6.6: Progress-tracking guide.

*Visit **go.SolutionTree.com/educatorwellness** for a free reproducible version of this figure.*

or your own observations if you were able to observe the teacher either face to face, virtually, or from a recorded lesson that the teacher shared with you. This is an essential element of helping to improve a teacher's expertise in order to positively impact student achievement.

Video Reflection

We know that athletes watch game film in order to prepare for the next game or match. According to National Football League player Marc Lillibridge (2012), "Great coaches take the time to teach the correct techniques and to show players where they can improve." Instructional coaches can do the same with their teachers. Harvard's Center for Education Policy Research (CEPR) created Visibly Better (https://visiblybetter.cepr.harvard.edu/about), a project that promotes video for self-reflection and coaching in order to deepen reflection, improve feedback, and change the culture to ensure that effective instructional supports are in place for teachers.

As your teachers work on their growth goals, encourage them to record themselves in action. There's no need to record an entire day or an entire class period. Instead, they only need to capture the strategy or behavior that they're engaging in deliberate practice on (their area 6 growth goal). The reproducible guide on page 120 might be a starting place; you can modify it as needed.

Either prior to or during your meeting with the teacher, consider having him or her *rate him- or herself* on the scale before offering your own designation. This helps to empower teachers and offers you a glimpse into their own thinking. They can also offer up what they plan to do to reach the next level. It's also OK if they're not sure what to do next, though; that's why they have *you*!

Collaboration

In order to create opportunities for teachers to increase self-efficacy through collaboratively sharing skills and experiences, consider ways that you can truly collaborate *with* your teachers. Kosha Patel, an instructional coach in Missisquoi Valley School District in Vermont, collaborates with her teachers on their growth goals beyond simply setting the goal together, which helps them *both* learn and leave the coaching cycle feeling empowered. For example, Kosha worked with one teacher who wanted to become good at conferring with students. Together, they developed a Google Form to help the teacher keep conference notes and they both practiced using it in the teacher's classroom with all the students. After a few weeks, the teacher moved up the various levels of the scale that they created together and this strategy became an effective and easy-to-implement way to positively impact student achievement. Both Kosha and her teacher finished the coaching cycle feeling like they had learned something that they could also share with others in their PLC, particularly their respective collaborative teams (K. Patel, personal communication, September 27, 2020). When teachers understand that coaching is a partnership in which both the coach and the teacher learn from one another, the relationship is nourished and strengthened and they feel empowered.

Collective Efficacy

If we believe that by improving our own skills, we can in turn help students to achieve success, then we have the ingredients necessary to improve our expertise. Even more powerfully, if we, as coaches, can work to help *all* our teachers establish a sense of *collective efficacy*, or a belief that when we *all* work together, we can inspire growth and achievement for *all* students, we're tapping into education professor and researcher John Hattie's number one influencer on student achievement (Donohoo, Hattie, & Eells, 2018). According to Visible Learning (n.d.), "A school staff that believes it can collectively accomplish great things is vital for the health of a school and if they believe they can make a positive difference then they very likely will." PLC architects and experts Richard DuFour, Rebecca DuFour, Robert Eaker, Thomas W. Many, and Mike Mattos (2016) also highlight the importance of collective responsibility among teachers to ensure the success of their students.

As a coach, you can support a sense of collective efficacy among your teachers by recognizing that your instructional leadership correlates to the ability of teachers to collaborate for improvement (by emphasizing this and providing time for teachers to work together), helping to build relational trust among your teachers (see chapter 4, page 57, for examples of physical and institutional support that increases a sense of belonging and trust), allowing teachers to take control of their own professional learning (by allowing them to create their own growth goals), and modeling the language that promotes collective efficacy (Department of Education and Training Victoria, 2019). Encourage your teachers to ask, "What's working and what could be better?" The four critical questions of a PLC also help teachers collectively focus on how to make sure every student learns at high levels (DuFour et al., 2016).

1. What do students need to know and be able to do?

2. How will we know when they have learned it?

3. What will we do when they haven't learned it?

4. What will we do when they already know it?

Additionally, the PLC process creates the perfect opportunity for teachers to share their skills and experiences (DuFour et al., 2016). There may be opportunities for you to work with entire collaborative teams in addition to meeting with individual teachers. Remember, the same principles that work with individual teachers also apply to teams: you must work hard to establish trust with all team members, you need to ask good questions, you should listen like heaven, work to empathize with their challenges, and help teams use their collective efficacy in order to build their instructional knowledge and skills using a developmental scale.

As teachers, both individually and collectively, meet their goals, be sure to celebrate and share these successes among the staff and then help the teacher or team select a new goal to work on. Doing so emphasizes continual growth and improvement. As educators, we never arrive at a destination and stop learning and growing; instead, we continually work to increase our expertise in the name of improving student achievement. (To note, this is also true for you as a coach and a leader.)

Generalized and Specialized Supports for New Educators

You'll be the one guiding the instructional support for those new to the teaching profession as you work to help them build instructional knowledge and skills. There are generalized supports that are good for your new teacher cohort as a whole—for these supports, you might be able to enlist other staff members to help—and there are specialized supports that are tailored to meet the skill level of each individual teacher, which you should provide. Please consider the following examples, and add your own thinking as well.

Generalized supports include the following.

- **Ensure that new teachers have necessary instructional materials:** This type of support overlaps the physical support that coaches provide during the Anticipation phase. Instructional materials include curriculum guides, proficiency scales, textbooks, supplemental materials, teacher guides, unit resources, manipulatives, and so on.

- **Offer group sessions for all new teachers centered around common needs:** These group sessions might include things like preparing for back-to-school night, parent- or student-led conferences, observations, formal assessments, instructional rounds, data-tracking meetings, lesson and unit planning, and so on. Opportunities to gather can be particularly helpful for your new teachers in order to increase a sense of belonging. You can create a monthly calendar with timely topics to address each month while also allowing some open time for issues that come up unexpectedly.

- **Set up shadowing opportunities:** This is invaluable in helping new teachers empathize with their students. Turn back to chapter 2 (page 29) to review this type of support. Here, teachers will shadow a student for a day and reflect on their learning and experience.

✒ **Arrange time for new teachers to observe effective experienced teachers:** Just like it's helpful to watch someone perform a skill that you're working on, it's helpful for new teachers to watch more experienced colleagues teach well. Guide the new teacher in what to watch for and debrief each observation, using reflection questions such as the following.

○ What did I see that I want to incorporate into my own classroom?

○ What questions do I have for my coach about what I observed?

○ What am I reflecting on regarding my own teaching practices?

✒ **Encourage reflection time:** Be careful not to overwhelm here. Offer a variety of reflection methods and questions that appeal to different personalities. For example, offer ways to reflect via writing, audio, or video and allow teachers to choose what appeals to them personally. Encourage new teachers to reflect on their specific growth goals as well as their self-care and wellness and general attitudes toward teaching throughout the year.

What are some generalized supports you might offer?

_____

_____

_____

_____

_____

_____

_____

_____

_____

_____

Specialized supports include the following.

- **Ensure one-to-one time with new teachers to address their specific needs:** You'll want to observe teachers either in person or via a video or Zoom class recording so that you can pinpoint what to celebrate as well as areas of focus or feedback in relation to the pedagogy-specific growth goals that you've helped the teacher create. Be sure to keep your feedback focused and be specific in your comments and questions rather than overwhelming teachers with too many strategies to tackle at one time. It's OK and appropriate to address areas of concern, but tackle these in small doses while also pointing out celebrations and areas of growth.

- **Allow time for new teachers to share any challenges they're facing:** Listen like heaven here so that you can provide targeted support that matches teachers' immediate needs. Remind them that your role is to help and support, not to evaluate or judge. Create a safe space for open and honest dialogue and conversation. Allow teachers to vent, but also nudge them toward solutions and remind them that they have the power to make changes.

- **Provide over-the-shoulder coaching for teachers who are struggling:** This could be via co-teaching or an *I do-you do* strategy (the same general idea as the gradual release of responsibility; Fisher & Frey, 2008) where teachers watch you engage in a strategy or entire lesson before trying it on their own. Be sure to reflect using the developmental scale and support the teacher so that he or she can move up through the various levels in order to reach proficiency in relation to one strategy at a time.

- **Model and provide video examples of instructional strategies:** It's often much easier to see a strategy in action than to read about a strategy in a book. Establish a library of video clips that mirror your instructional model or locate videos online that help demonstrate the strategy that you're working on.

    Provide actionable feedback: Your goal is to help the new teacher know the next step to engage in deliberate practice on by using the scale and progress-tracking resources outlined earlier in this chapter.

What are some specialized supports you might offer?

_____
_____
_____
_____
_____
_____
_____
_____
_____
_____

Generalized and Specialized Instructional Support for Experienced Teachers

Instructional support is essential for *all* teachers, no matter how long they have taught. Yet, it is essential that you recognize how coaching experienced teachers is different than coaching novice teachers. Start by making a conscious effort to truly honor and respect the expertise of your veteran staff. Shadowing their day-to-day teaching life is a solid starting place (as suggested in chapter 2, page 29) as it builds empathy for their challenges.

Another way to honor your veteran teachers' expertise is to tap into their skills as a way to support your new teachers. Doing this not only helps new teachers but also gives experienced teachers a shot of motivation they might really desire: knowing that someone else needs them. They don't have to take on the burden of organizing and disseminating the valuable resource that is their experience, though—you (or someone you delegate the task to) will take care of that. Record their expert use of strategies to add to your library of resources and request copies of particularly thoughtful lesson plans, communication with parents, substitute plans, project ideas, and so on. Strive to continually build a solid partnership with your experienced teachers by highlighting their expertise both publicly and privately. Use your listening like heaven skills when you're with your veterans just like you do with your newbies. Eventually, once you've built a solid relationship with a foundation of mutual respect, offer up ways that you can provide additional instructional support. As always, your goal here is to move teachers from where they are to where they want to be; consider the honor that it is to do this for someone else.

You might create a menu of options for ways you can support your experienced teachers, bearing in mind that different schools and districts have varying expectations around the role of a coach, so you should select the strategies that work for your particular situation. Such menu options could include the following.

- Plan a new unit or lesson together.
- Develop curriculum, assessments, materials, surveys, and so on.
- Support a small group of students while the teacher works with another group of students.
- Co-teach a new lesson.
- Act as an accountability partner for educator wellness goals.
- Help set up peer coaching opportunities with other staff members who share similar goals.
- Act as a safe sounding board if your teacher's style is to talk through issues, ideas, or concerns.
- Help analyze data and act as a data coach.
- Record a lesson or part of a lesson for self-reflection and analysis.
- Co-create student surveys in order to gain additional feedback in relation to growth goals.
- Support technology growth.

Other ways that you can provide instructional support for your entire staff might include the following.

- Run professional development during faculty meetings, lunchtime learning sessions, coffee talks, department presentations, full and half professional development days, after-school sessions, and so on.

- Examine student work together.

- Arrange and support lesson study groups.

- Act as the lead for instructional rounds or cover classes so teachers can participate in rounds.

- Research and curate educational briefs to share and discuss with the staff.

- Provide up-to-date research and literature reviews.

- Create newsletters and resources for teachers.

- Create websites of linked and downloadable resources for both teachers and families.

- Act as the social media specialist, promoting the positive activities in classrooms and at school.

- Collaborate with other coaches in order to continually build your own expertise.

- Act as the morale booster—particularly during the disillusionment phase.

- Promote (and model) educator wellness.

- Seek out conferences and workshops that are relevant to the school or individual goals and encourage others to attend.

- Encourage teacher leadership by seeking out opportunities for teachers to shine, such as presenting at a staff meeting or at education conferences.

- Secure books and set up book clubs or book studies around particular topics of interest.

We must always hold high expectations for students. And the same is true of the teachers we serve. Supporting them is an essential and honorable mission, and we will always, always need instructional coaches to help lead the way, particularly when it comes to providing targeted instructional support. When teachers have this support, they can perform at their best and, in turn, our students will benefit and achieve their very best.

Helping your teachers to improve their pedagogical skills in support of student achievement is one of the most important roles you will take on as an instructional coach. As you continue to refine your skills in this area, take time to reflect on the following questions.

reflection questions

1   Do you and your administrative team have the same vision for your role as an instructional leader? How do you know? How can you ensure that you share a common vision?

_____

_____

_____

_____

_____

_____

_____

2   How do you or can you establish and promote both self-efficacy and collective efficacy for your teachers?

_____

_____

_____

_____

_____

_____

_____

3   How do you differentiate your instructional support for new teachers versus veteran teachers?

_____

_____

_____

_____

_____

_____

_____

notes

Guidelines for Encouraging
Teacher Self-Reflection

1. Review the teacher's growth goals and how the scale reflects growth in the chosen areas. Ask the teacher to video record him- or herself working on the goal in class and to articulate how the clip demonstrates his or her growth goals.

2. While watching the video (and before meeting with the teacher), consider the following.

   ○ What can you celebrate?

   _____

   _____

   _____

   _____

   _____

   ○ Identify at what level of the scale the teacher currently is and why (be sure to cite specific teacher and student evidence here).

   _____

   _____

   _____

   _____

   _____

   ○ Consider how you will coach this teacher to move to the next level (focusing on just one level at a time). What does growth look like? Use examples of both teacher and student evidence here.

   _____

   _____

   _____

   _____

   _____

Epilogue

It was an honor to write this book for you. As I imagined you, my reader, I smiled, because I can picture you digging into these pages with sincere interest and engagement, highlighting passages that resonate with you and making plans as to how to implement new ideas into your repertoire of tools—because you're a coach, and that's what good coaches do. Seriously, you're the best.

Choosing to leave the classroom and enter the world of coaching is a huge change. Most coaches never knew they'd end up here. I certainly didn't. We usually start out as teachers and imagine ourselves teaching our current students' children and grandchildren, but then we get that nudge, maybe from a mentor or an administrator, someone who says, "Hey, you're good at this teaching thing, can you help others do a bit more of what you do?" Or maybe you've worked with an outstanding coach yourself and thought, *I'd like to do that for people; that's a pretty incredible gift.* Whatever the case may be, we're lucky you're here. We need you.

As I write this, during the 2020–2021 school year, the education landscape is shifting under our feet. And while we don't know exactly what our schools will look like on the other side of this pandemic, we do know that they will be forever changed from this moment on. In fact, that's the main challenge of our field: it's *always* changing. It was changing before the COVID-19 pandemic, and it will continue to change year after year, even as we start to adjust to the unique challenges and opportunities of this particular time. As instructional coaches, our mission is to remain steady and to help our teachers stand on solid ground themselves. We can feel safe that the core tenets of the essential supports outlined in this text will remain true while the specific strategies associated with the supports may shift as schools adjust to the current landscape.

As education consultant and author Elena Aguilar (2013) so eloquently states:

> Coaching can build will, skill, knowledge, and capacity because it can go where no other professional development has gone before: into the intellect, behaviors, practices, beliefs, values, and feelings of an educator. Coaching creates a relationship in which a client feels cared for and is therefore able to access and implement new knowledge. A coach can foster conditions in which deep reflection and learning can take place, where a teacher can take risks to change her practice, where powerful conversations can take place and where growth is recognized and celebrated. Finally, a coach holds a space where healing can take place and where resilient, joyful communities can be built. (p. 8)

As you continually work to improve your craft as a coach, consider how you can collect meaningful feedback from your teachers and teams. You might survey them a few times a year (being considerate of their time) and also look at formative student assessment data in order to pinpoint what's working and what isn't so you can both celebrate and offer guidance around meaningful growth goals. I also encourage you to reach out to other instructional coaches in order to support one another, whether that's by sharing new strategies or simply having a safe place to vent frustrations and challenges. Always, always model what you want to see in your teachers and promise me that you'll take exquisite care of yourself along the way, too.

You've got what you need. Take a moment to revisit chapter 1 (page 9), and remind yourself of your greater why and those essential values that will serve to guide you in this work. Be gentle with yourself and remember that expertise takes times—yes, this includes coaches, too. Remember to put your own oxygen mask on first; your staff is looking to you to lead by example—do it well.

References and Resources

Achor, S. (2010). *The happiness advantage: The seven principles of positive psychology that fuel success and performance at work.* New York: Broadway Books.

Adams, W., Pineda, A., Gomez, J., Yoshiaki, T., Fratantuno, M., & Pajon, G. (2003). Let's get it started [Recorded by Black Eyed Peas]. On *Elephunk* [CD]. Santa Monica, CA: A & M Records.

Aguilar, E. (2013). *The art of coaching: Effective strategies for school transformation.* San Francisco: Jossey-Bass.

American Federation of Teachers. (2017). *2017 educator quality of work life survey.* Washington, DC: American Federation of Teachers and Badass Teachers Association. Accessed at www .aft.org/sites/default/files/2017_eqwl_survey_web.pdf on January 26, 2021.

Anderson, R. (2012). *A fascinating new concept: How "thought partners" add value to your business.* Accessed at www.forbes.com/sites /barbarastanny/2012/06/19/a-fascinating-new-concept-how -thought-partners-add-value-to-your-business/ on March 15, 2021.

Arzón, R. (2016). *Shut up and run: How to get up, lace up, and sweat with swagger.* New York: Harper Design.

Banks, O. (2019, January 8). *Alternatives to setting SMART goals.* Accessed at https://projectmanagersuccess.com/career/smart -goals-alternatives/ on October 30, 2020.

Barile, N. (2019, October 22). 6 ways teachers can ease decision fatigue. *Hey Teach!* Accessed at www.wgu.edu/heyteach/article /6-ways-teachers-can-ease-decision-fatigue1910.html on March 16, 2021.

Baumeister, R. F., & Tierney, J. (2011). *Willpower: Rediscovering the greatest human strength.* New York: Penguin.

Boodman, S. G. (2015, March 12). Efforts to instill empathy among doctors are paying dividends. *Kaiser Health News.* Accessed at https://khn.org/news/efforts-to-instill-empathy-among-doctors-is -paying-dividends/ on March 11, 2021.

Boogren, T. H. (2015). *Supporting beginning teachers.* Bloomington, IN: Marzano Resources.

Boogren, T. H. (2018). *Take time for you: Self-care action plans for educators.* Bloomington, IN: Solution Tree Press.

Boogren, T. H. (2020). *180 days of self-care for busy educators.* Bloomington, IN: Solution Tree Press.

Brinson, D., & Steiner, L. (2007). *Building collective efficacy: How leaders inspire teachers to achieve.* Accessed at https://files.eric.ed.gov/fulltext/ED499254.pdf on November 3, 2020.

Brooks, A. W., & John, L. K. (2018). *The surprising power of questions.* Accessed at hbr.org/2018/05/the-surprising-power-of-questions on October 30, 2020.

Brown, B. (2018). *Dare to lead: Brave work, tough conversations, whole hearts.* New York: Random House.

Brown, J. (1965). I got you (I feel good). On *I got you (I feel good)* [Vinyl record]. Cincinnati, OH: King.

Burns, J. M. (1979). *Leadership.* New York: Perennial.

BusyTeacher.org. (n.d.). *Teachers: The real masters of multitasking.* Accessed at http://busyteacher.org/16670-teacher-masters-of-multitasking-infographic.html on October 30, 2020.

Cain, J., Perry, S., & Schon, N. (1981). Don't stop believin' [Recorded by Journey]. On *Escape* [CD]. New York: Columbia.

Center for Educational Leadership. (n.d.). *5 dimensions of teaching and learning.* Accessed at http://info.k-12leadership.org/5-dimensions-of-teaching-and-learning on November 2, 2020.

Centers for Disease Control and Prevention. (2020, April 13). *About the CDC-Kaiser ACE Study.* Accessed at https://www.cdc.gov/violenceprevention/aces/about.html on October 30, 2020.

Cherry, K. (2020). *How do transformational leaders inspire and motivate followers?* Accessed at www.verywellmind.com/what-is-transformational-leadership-2795313 on March 16, 2021.

Chiang, E. (2018). *20 scavenger hunt ideas for adults.* Accessed at www.goosechase.com/blog/planning-a-scavenger-hunt-for-adults/ on November 3, 2020.

Choi, S. L., Goh, C. F., Adam, M. B., & Tan, O. K. (2016). Transformational leadership, empowerment, and job satisfaction: The mediating role of employee empowerment. *Human Resources for Health, 14*(1), 73.

Clear, J. (n.d.a). *The 1 percent rule: Why a few people get most of the rewards.* Accessed at http://jamesclear.com/the-1-percent-rule on March 16, 2021.

Clear, J. (n.d.b). *The beginner's guide to deliberate practice.* Accessed at https://jamesclear.com/beginners-guide-deliberate-practice on October 30, 2020.

Clear, J. (n.d.c). *Core values list.* Accessed at https://jamesclear.com/core-values on March 10, 2021.

Clear, J. (n.d.d). *How willpower works: How to avoid bad decisions.* Accessed at https://jamesclear.com/willpower-decision-fatigue on October 30, 2020.

Clear, J. (2018). *Atomic habits: An easy and proven way to build good habits and break bad ones.* London, UK: Penguin Random House UK.

Coe, D. A. (1977). Take this job and shove it [Recorded by Johnny Paycheck]. On *Take this job and shove it* [Vinyl record]. New York: Epic.

Cole, N. (2016, September 24). *10 fundamental things people don't understand about practice.* Accessed at www.inc.com/nicolas-cole/10-fundamental-things-people-dont-understand-about-practice.html on March 16, 2021.

Conzemius, A., & O'Neill, J. (2014). *The handbook for SMART school teams: Revitalizing best practices for collaboration* (2nd ed.). Bloomington, IN: Solution Tree Press.

Cooper, A., Bruce, M., Buxton, G., Dunaway, D., & Smith, N. (1972). School's out [Recorded by Alice Cooper]. On *School's out* [CD]. Los Angeles: Warner.

Covey, S. M. R. (2006). *The speed of trust: The one thing that changes everything.* New York: Free Press.

Coyle, D. (2018). *The culture code: The secrets of highly successful groups.* New York: Penguin Random House.

Cuban, L. (2011, June 16). *Jazz, basketball, and teacher decision-making.* http://larrycuban.wordpress.com/2011/06/16/jazz-basketball-and-teacher-decision-making/ on March 16, 2021.

Damasio, A. R. (1995). *Descartes' error: Emotion, reason, and the human brain.* New York: Penguin.

Danielson Group. (n.d.). *The framework for teaching.* Accessed at https://danielsongroup.org/framework/framework-teaching on October 30, 2020.

Dawson, G. (2017, August 27). *How decision fatigue ruins your day (and how to beat it)*. Accessed at www.cultofpedagogy.com /teacher-decision-fatigue on March 16, 2021.

Department of Education and Training Victoria. (2019). *Developing collective efficacy*. Accessed at www.education.vic.gov.au/school /teachers/teachingresources/discipline/english/Pages/developing -collective-efficacy.aspx.

Diliberti, M. K., Schwartz, H. L., & Grant, D. (2021). *Stress topped the reasons why public school teachers quit, even before COVID-19*. Santa Monica, CA: RAND Corporation. Accessed at www.rand .org/pubs/research_reports/RRA1121-2.html on March 16, 2021.

Dillard, T., Gottwald, L., Walter, H., Isaac, B., Pournouri, A., Bergling, T., et al. (2012). Good feeling [Recorded by Flo Rida]. On *Wild ones* [CD]. New York: Poe Boy Music/Atlantic.

Donohoo, J., Hattie, J., & Eells, R. (2018). The power of collective efficacy. *Educational Leadership*, *75*(6), 40–44.

DuFour, R., DuFour, R., Eaker, R., Many, T. W., & Mattos, M. (2016). *Learning by doing: A handbook for Professional Learning Communities at Work* (3rd ed.). Bloomington, IN: Solution Tree Press.

Eaker, R., & Marzano, R. J. (Eds.) (2020). *Professional Learning Communities at Work and High Reliability Schools: Cultures of continuous learning*. Bloomington, IN: Solution Tree Press.

Ericsson, A., & Pool, R. (2016). *Peak: Secrets from the new science of expertise*. New York: Mariner.

Ericsson, K. A., Prietula, M. J., & Cokely, E. T. (2007). *The making of an expert*. Accessed at http://hbr.org/2007/07/the-making-of -an-expert on October 30, 2020.

Fisher, D., & Frey, N. (2008). *Better learning through structured teaching: A framework for the gradual release of responsibility*. Alexandria, VA: Association for Supervision and Curriculum Development.

Fuller, R. (2013, December 18). *Teaching isn't rocket science. It's harder*. Accessed at https://slate.com/human-interest/2013/12/teaching -in-americas-highest-need-communities-isnt-rocket-science-its -harder.html on October 30, 2020.

Gilbert, E. (2015). *Big magic: Creative living beyond fear*. New York: Riverhead Books.

Goldberg, G., & Houser, R. (2017, July 19). *Battling decision fatigue*. Accessed at www.edutopia.org/blog/battling-decision-fatigue -gravity-goldberg-renee-houser on March 16, 2021.

Gonzalez, J. (2014, June 7). *The gut-level teacher reflection*. Accessed at https://www.cultofpedagogy.com/gut-level-reflection-questions/ on October 2020.

Gonzalez, J. (2015, May 27). *Goal-setting for teachers: 8 paths to self-improvement*. Accessed at https://www.cultofpedagogy.com/goal-setting-for-teachers/ on October 30, 2020.

Griffith, R., Bauml, M., & Quebec-Fuentes, S. (2016). Promoting metacognitive decision-making in teacher education. *Theory Into Practice, 55*(3), 242–249.

Harrison, C., & Killion, J. (2007). Ten roles for teacher leaders. *Educational Leadership, 65*(1), 74–77. Accessed at www.ascd.org/publications/educational-leadership/sept07/vol65/num01/Ten-Roles-for-Teacher-Leaders.aspx on November 2, 2020.

Henson, W. (2020). *4 key pillars of a trauma-informed approach during COVID-19*. Accessed at www.eschoolnews.com/2020/12/17/4-key-pillars-of-a-trauma-informed-approach-during-covid-19/2/ on March 16, 2021.

Higdon, H. (2005). *Marathon: The ultimate training guide* (3rd ed.). Emmaus, PA: Rodale.

Hill, P. L., Sin, N. L, Turiano, N. A., Burrow, A. L., & Almeida, D. M. (2018). A sense of purpose moderates the associations between daily stressors and daily well-being. *History Studies International Journal of History, 10*(7), 241–264.

Hills, J. (2018). *How an understanding of neuroscience can help create inclusion*. Accessed at https://heaheartbrain.com/resources/how-an-understanding-of-neuroscience-can-help-create-inclusion on March 16, 2021.

Hoomans, J. (2015). *35,000 decisions: The great choices of strategic leaders*. Accessed at https://go.roberts.edu/leadingedge/the-great-choices-of-strategic-leaders on November 2, 2020.

Jackson, C. K. (2018). What do test scores miss?: The importance of teacher effects on non–test score outcomes. *Journal of Political Economy, 126*(5). Accessed at www.journals.uchicago.edu/doi/10.1086/699018 on March 16, 2021.

Jacobs, C., Pfaff, H., Lehner, B., Driller, E., Nitzsche, A., Stieler-Lorenz, B., et al. (2013). The influence of transformational leadership on employee well-being: Results from a survey of companies in the information and communication technology sector in Germany, *Journal of Occupational and Environmental Medicine, 55*(7), 772–778.

James, B., Lindsey, H., & Sampson, G. (2005). Jesus, take the wheel [Recorded by Carrie Underwood]. On *Some hearts* [CD]. New York: Arista.

Jeffrey, S. (n.d.). *Core values list: Over 200 personal values to discover what's most important to you.* Accessed at https://scottjeffrey.com /core-values-list/ on March 10, 2021.

Keels, M. (2018). *Supporting students with chronic trauma.* Accessed at www.edutopia.org/article/supporting-students-chronic-trauma on March 16, 2021.

Kelly, M. (2019, November 7). *Can administrators be coaches? Yes and no.* Accessed at https://instructionalcoaching.com/can -administrators-be-coaches-yes-and-no/ on November 2, 2020.

Khaer, D. E. (2020). *How minimalism helps you overcome decision fatigue.* Accessed at http://medium.com/change-your-mind/how -minimalism-helps-you-overcome-decision-fatigue-b815cad702af on March 16, 2021.

Knight, J. (2013). *High-impact instruction: A framework for great teaching.* Thousand Oaks, CA: Corwin Press.

Knight, J. (2016). *Better conversations: Coaching ourselves and each other to be more credible, caring, and contented.* Thousand Oaks, CA: Corwin Press.

Kreek, A. (2020, November 23). *CLEAR goals are better than SMART goals.* Accessed at www.kreekspeak.com/clear-goal-setting on March 16, 2021.

Lamothe, C. (2019, October 30). *Understanding decision fatigue.* Accessed at www.healthline.com/health/decision-fatigue on March 16, 2021.

Lamott, A. (1994). *Bird by bird: Some instructions on writing and life.* New York: Pantheon Books.

Leadership. (n.d.). In *Dictionary.com.* Accessed at www.dictionary .com/browse/leadership?s=t on January 19, 2021.

Lennon, J., & McCartney, P. (1965). Yesterday [Recorded by the Beatles]. On *Help!* [CD]. London: Parlophone.

Lillibridge, M. (2012). *A former player's perspective on film study and preparing for an NFL game.* Accessed at https://bleacherreport .com/articles/1427449-a-former-players-perspective-on-film -study-and-preparing-for-a-nfl-game on November 2, 2020.

Lipton, L., & Wellman, B. (2017). *Mentoring matters: A practical guide to learning-focused relationships* (3rd ed.). Sherman, CT: MiraVia.

Locke, E. A., Cartledge, N., & Knerr, C. S. (1970). Studies of the relationship between satisfaction, goal-setting, and performance. *Organizational Behavior and Human Performance, 5*(2), 135–158.

Lopez-Garrido, G. (2020, August 9). *Self-efficacy theory.* Accessed at www.simplypsychology.org/self-efficacy.html on March 16, 2021.

Lynch, M. (2016, June 9). *Ask an expert: The effects of teacher burnout.* Accessed at https://www.theedadvocate.org/ask-dr-lynch-the -effects-of-teacher-burnout/ on November 2, 2020.

MacCrindle, A., & Duginske, J. (2018, April 5). *Seven qualities of an instructional coach.* Accessed at https://inservice.ascd.org/seven -qualities-of-an-instructional-coach/ on November 2, 2020.

Marzano, R. J. (2012). *Becoming a reflective teacher.* Bloomington, IN: Marzano Resources.

Marzano, R. J. (2017). *The new art and science of teaching.* Bloomington, IN: Solution Tree Press.

Marzano, R. J., Frontier, T., & Livingston, D. (2011). *Effective supervision: Supporting the art and science of teaching.* Alexandria, VA: Association for Supervision and Curriculum Development.

Marzano, R. J., Rains, C. L., & Warrick, P. B. (2020) *Improving teacher development and evaluation: A guide for leaders, coaches, and teachers.* Bloomington, IN: Marzano Resources.

Marzano, R. J., Scott, D., Boogren, T. H., & Newcomb, M. L. (2017). *Motivating and inspiring students: Strategies to awaken the learner.* Bloomington, IN: Marzano Resources.

Marzano, R. J., & Simms, J. A. (2013). *Coaching classroom instruction.* Bloomington, IN: Marzano Resources.

Maslow, A. H. (1943). A theory of human motivation. *Psychological Review, 50*(4), 370–396.

Maslow, A. H. (1969). The farther reaches of human nature. *Journal of Transpersonal Psychology, 1*(1), 1-9.

Mayo Clinic. (2019, April 5). *Stress relief from laughter? It's no joke.* Accessed at www.mayoclinic.org/healthy-lifestyle/stress -management/in-depth/stress-relief/art-20044456 on March 16, 2021.

McCarthy, J. (2018, January 10). *Extending the silence.* Accessed at www.edutopia.org/article/extending-silence on March 16, 2021.

Mesh, J. (2018, February 21). *How to beat decision fatigue with better brain habits* [Blog post]. Accessed at https://blog.trello.com/beat -decision-fatigue-with-better-brain-habits on November 2, 2020.

Miller, C. C. (n.d.). *How to be more empathetic.* Accessed at www
.nytimes.com/guides/year-of-living-better/how-to-be-more
-empathetic on March 16, 2021.

Minahan, J. (2019). Trauma-informed teaching strategies. *Making
School a Safe Place, 77*(2), 30–35. Accessed at www.ascd.org
/publications/educational_leadership/oct19/vol77/num02/Trauma
-Informed_Teaching_Strategies.aspx on November 2, 2020.

Moir, E. (1999). The stages of a teacher's first year. In M. Scherer
(Ed.), *A better beginning: Supporting and mentoring new teachers*
(pp. 19–23). Alexandria, VA: Association for Supervision and
Curriculum Development.

Moir, E. (2011, August). *Phases of first-year teaching.* Santa Cruz, CA:
New Teacher Center.

Molenberghs, P. (2020, June 11). *Understanding others' feelings: What is
empathy and why do we need it?* Accessed at http://theconversation
.com/understanding-others-feelings-what-is-empathy-and-why
-do-we-need-it-68494 on March 16, 2021.

Morrison, J., Manzarek, R., Krieger, R., & Densmore, J. (1967).
The end [Recorded by the Doors]. On *The Doors* [Vinyl record].
Burbank, CA: Elektra.

Muhammad, A. (2011, September 21). *Important model PLC update.*
Accessed at www.allthingsplc.info/blog/view/143/developing-a
-shared-mission on March 16, 2021.

Murphy, M. (2017). *HARD Goals, not SMART Goals, are the
key to career development.* Accessed at www.forbes.com/sites
/markmurphy/2017/06/11/hard-goals-not-smart-goals-are-the
-key-to-career-development/#1ea36a3070fb on November
2, 2020.

Neer, M. (2014, August 5). *The path to automaticity for teachers*
[Blog post]. Accessed at https://dataworks-ed.com/blog/2014
/08/the-path-to-automaticity-for-teachers/ on March 15, 2021.

Opper, I. M. (2019). *Teachers matter: Understanding teachers' impact
on student achievement.* Santa Monica, CA: RAND Corporation.
Accessed at www.rand.org/pubs/research_reports/RR4312.html
on March 16, 2021.

Palahniuk, C. (1999). *Invisible monsters.* New York: W. W. Norton
& Company.

Pasricha, N. (2016). *The happiness equation: Want nothing + do
anything = have everything.* New York: Penguin.

Phair, R. (2020, December 18). *COVID has worsened student adversity and trauma: How can schools help?* Accessed at http://oecdedutoday.com/covid-has-worsened-student -adversity-trauma-how-schools-help on March 16, 2021.

Pointer, A., Pointer, J., Pointer, R., & Lawrence, T. (1982). I'm so excited [Recorded by the Pointer Sisters]. On *So excited!* [Vinyl record]. New York: Planet.

Price, O. A., & Ellis, W. (2018, February 26). *Student trauma is widespread: Schools don't have to go it alone.* Accessed at www .edweek.org/leadership/opinion-student-trauma-is-widespread -schools-dont-have-to-go-it-alone/2018/02 on March 16, 2021.

Purkey, W. W., & Novak, J. M. (1996). *Inviting school success: A self-concept approach to teaching, learning, and democratic practice* (3rd ed.). Florence, KY: Wadsworth.

Purkey, W. W., & Novak, J. M. (2015, September). *An introduction to invitational theory.* Accessed at www.invitationaleducation.org/wp -content/uploads/2019/04/art_intro_to_invitational_theory-1.pdf on March 16, 2021.

Rao, S. (2019, July 22). *Three simple habits that boost your happiness, according to science.* Accessed at https://nextbigideaclub.com /conversation-three-simple-habits-that-boost-your-happiness -according-to-science/21328/?utm_source=newsletter_the _lift&utm_campaign=072919 on October 30, 2020.

Riley-Missouri, C. (2018, April 24). *Lots of teachers are super stressed out.* Accessed at https://futurity.org/teachers-stress-1739832 on January 25, 2021.

Robbins, M. (2018). *The five elements of the 5 second rule.* Accessed at https://melrobbins.com/blog/five-elements-5-second-rule/ on November 2, 2020.

Rowe, M. B. (1972, April). *Wait-time and rewards as instructional variables: Their influence on language, logic, and fate control.* Paper presented at the National Association for Research in Science Teaching, Chicago, IL.

Schön, D. A. (1983). *The reflective practitioner: How professionals think in action.* New York: Basic Books.

Seehausen, M., Kazzer, P., Bajbouj, M., & Prehn, K. (2012). Effects of empathic paraphrasing: Extrinsic emotion regulation in social conflict. *Frontiers in Psychology.* Accessed at www.ncbi.nlm.nih .gov/pmc/articles/PMC3495333 on March 16, 2021.

Sparks, S. D. (2011). *Study finds late-hired teachers likely to leave.* Accessed at https://www.edweek.org/ew/articles/2011/03/16 /24hire_ep.h30.html on November 2, 2020.

Sparks, S. D. (2017). *How teachers' stress affects students: A research roundup.* Accessed at https://www.edweek.org/tm/articles/2017 /06/07/how-teachers-stress-affects-students-a-research.html on November 2, 2020.

Springsteen, B. (1984). Glory days. On *Born in the U.S.A.* [CD]. New York: Columbia.

Stanier, M. B. (2016). *The coaching habit: Say less, ask more, and change the way you lead forever.* Toronto, Canada: Box of Crayons Press.

Sutcher, L., Darling-Hammond, L., & Carver-Thomas, D. (2016). *A coming crisis in teaching? Teacher supply, demand, and shortages in the U.S.* Palo Alto, CA: Learning Policy Institute.

Suttie, J. (2017, July 17). *How laughter brings us together.* Accessed at https://greatergood.berkeley.edu/article/item/how_laughter _brings_us_together on October 30, 2020.

Tate, E. (2020). *Survey: Nearly half of teachers have recently considered a job change as COVID-19 drags on.* Accessed at www.edsurge.com /news/2020-08-31-survey-nearly-half-of-teachers-have-recently -considered-a-job-change-as-covid-19-drags-on on March 15, 2021.

Tierney, J. (2011, August 17). *Do you suffer from decision fatigue?* Accessed at www.nytimes.com/2011/08/21/magazine/do-you -suffer-from-decision-fatigue.html on November 2, 2020.

Vedder, E. (2009). Just breathe [Recorded by Pearl Jam]. On *Backspacer* [CD]. Seattle, WA: Monkeywrench.

Visible Learning. (n.d.). *Collective teacher efficacy (CTE) according to John Hattie.* Accessed at https://visible-learning.org/2018/03 /collective-teacher-efficacy-hattie/ on March 15, 2021.

Walker, T. (2018, May 11). *How many teachers are highly stressed? Maybe more than people think.* Accessed at www.nea.org /advocating-for-change/new-from-nea/how-many-teachers-are -highly-stressed-maybe-more-people-think on January 18, 2021.

West-Rosenthal, L. B. (2017, August 11). *6 easy ways to welcome new teachers and support staff.* Accessed at https://www.weareteachers .com/easy-ways-to-welcome-new-teachers-support-staff/ on November 2, 2020.

Will, M. (2021, February 22). *Teachers are stressed out, and it's causing some to quit.* Accessed at www.edweek.org/teaching-learning /teachers-are-stressed-out-and-its-causing-some-to-quit/2021/02 on March 16, 2021.

Williams, P. (2014). Happy. On *GIRL* [CD]. New York: Columbia.

Winfrey, O. (n.d.). *What Oprah knows for sure about gratitude.* Accessed at http://www.oprah.com/spirit/oprahs-gratitude -journal-oprah-on-gratitude on November 2, 2020.

Yong, E. (2016, January 5). *The incredible thing we do during conversations.* Accessed at www.theatlantic.com/science/archive/2016/01/the -incredible-thing-we-do-during-conversations/422439/ on March 16, 2021.

Young, A., Young, M., & Scott, B. (1979). Highway to hell [Recorded by AC/DC]. On *Highway to hell* [Vinyl record]. New York: Atlantic.

Index

The Beginning Teacher's Field Guide:
Tina H. Boogren
The joys and pains of starting a teaching career often go undiscussed. This guide explores the personal side of teaching, offering crucial advice and support. The author details six phases every new teacher goes through and outlines classroom strategies and self-care practices.
BKF806

Take Time for You
Tina H. Boogren
The key to thriving as a human and an educator rests in self-care. With _Take Time for You_, you'll discover a clear path to well-being. The author offers manageable strategies, reflection questions, and surveys that will guide you in developing an individualized self-care plan.
BKF813

180 Days of Self-Care for Busy Educators
Tina H. Boogren
Rely on _180 Days of Self-Care for Busy Educators_ to help you lead a happier, healthier more fulfilled life inside and outside of the classroom. With Tina H. Boogren's guidance, you will work through 36 weeks of self-care strategies during the school year.
BKF920

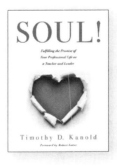

SOUL!
Timothy D. Kanold
Chart a deeply rewarding journey toward discovering your soul story—the pursuit of your moral good, to create good in others. Refreshing and uplifting, this resource includes dozens of real stories from educators, as well as ample space for journaling and self-reflection.
BKF982

Solution Tree | Press

a division of
Solution Tree

Visit SolutionTree.com or call 800.733.6786 to order.

Wait! Your professional development journey doesn't have to end with the last pages of this book.

We realize improving student learning doesn't happen overnight. And your school or district shouldn't be left to puzzle out all the details of this process alone.

No matter where you are on the journey, we're committed to helping you get to the next stage.

Take advantage of everything from **custom workshops** to **keynote presentations** and **interactive web and video conferencing**. We can even help you develop an action plan tailored to fit your specific needs.

Let's get the conversation started.

Call 888.763.9045 today.

SolutionTree.com